The Siegfried Line 1944–45

Battles on the German frontier

Campaign • 181

The Siegfried Line 1944–45

Battles on the German frontier

Steven J Zaloga • Illustrated by Steve Noon

First published in 2007 by Osprey Publishing
Midland House, West Way, Botley, Oxford OX2 0PH, UK
443 Park Avenue South, New York, NY 10016, USA
E-mail: info@ospreypublishing.com

ISBN 978 1 84603 121 2

Design: The Black Spot
Index by Alison Worthington
Cartography: The Map Studio
Bird's-eye view artworks: Chris Taylor
Originated by PDQ Digital Media Solutions
Printed in China through Worldprint

07 08 09 10 11   10 9 8 7 6 5 4 3 2 1

A CIP catalog record for this book is available from the British Library.

For a catalog of all books by Osprey please contact:

NORTH AMERICA
Osprey Direct, 2427 Bond Street, University Park, IL 60466, USA
E-mail: info@ospreydirectusa.com

ALL OTHER REGIONS
Osprey Direct UK, P.O. Box 140, Wellingborough, Northants, NN8 2FA, UK
E-mail: info@ospreydirect.co.uk

Image credits

Unless otherwise indicated, the photos in this book are
from the collections of the US Army Signal Corps, located
at the US National Archives and Records Administration
(NARA) in College Park, MD and the US Army Military
History Institute (MHI), Carlisle Barracks, PA.

Author's note

The author would like to thank Timm Haasler for his help in
obtaining maps of the Westwall defenses around Aachen.
Thanks also go to the staff of the US Army's Military History
Institute (MHI) at the Army War College at Carlisle Barracks,
PA and the staff of the US National Archive, College Park
for their kind assistance in the preparation of this book.
For brevity, the traditional conventions have been used
when referring to units. In the case of US units, 1/179th
Infantry refers to the 1st Battalion, 179th Infantry Regiment.
In the case of German units GR 725 indicates Grenadier
Regiment 725. With regard to German place names, this
book uses the common English spelling of "Roer" for the
river called the "Rur" by the Germans.

Artist's note

Key to military symbols

×××××	××××	×××	××	×	|||	||
Army Group	Army	Corps	Division	Brigade	Regiment	Battalion
Company/Battery	Platoon	Section	Squad	Infantry	Artillery	Cavalry
Airborne	Unit HQ	Air defense	Air Force	Air mobile	Air transportable	Amphibious
Antitank	Armor	Air aviation	Bridging	Engineer	Headquarters	Maintenance
Medical	Missile	Mountain	Navy	Nuclear, biological, chemical	Ordnance	Parachute
Reconnaissance	Signal	Supply	Transport movement	Rocket artillery	Air defense artillery	

Key to unit identification

Unit identifier		Parent unit
	Commander	
	(+) with added elements	
	(-) less elements	

CONTENTS

INTRODUCTION 7

CHRONOLOGY 8

THE STRATEGIC SITUATION 9

OPPOSING COMMANDERS 13
German commanders • US commanders

OPPOSING ARMIES 16
The Wehrmacht • The US Army

OPPOSING PLANS 27
US plans • German plans

THE CAMPAIGN 31
The first battle of Aachen • North of Aachen
Encircling Aachen • The second battle of Aachen
Prelude to Operation *Queen*: Hürtgen • Operation *Queen*
Operation *Clipper*: VIII Corps • Operation *Queen*: the December clean up
The prelude to the Ardennes

THE CAMPAIGN IN RETROSPECT 91
The battlefields today

FURTHER READING 93

GLOSSARY AND ABBREVIATIONS 94

INDEX 95

INTRODUCTION

The western frontier of the Third Reich was protected by the Westwall fortifications, better known to the Allies as the Siegfried Line. The Allies began encountering the Siegfried Line in September 1944 after pursuing the retreating Wehrmacht through Belgium and the Netherlands. Fighting along the Westwall lasted for more than six months, with the final major operations in March 1945 in the Saar. All of the major Allied formations, including Montgomery's 21st Army Group, Bradley's 12th Army Group, and Devers' 6th Army Group, were involved at one time or another in fighting against the Westwall defenses. However, the focus of this book is on the most concentrated and intense fighting along the Siegfried Line by the US First and Ninth armies, the campaign that epitomizes the grim battles along the German frontier. Given its nature as a historic invasion route towards Germany's industrial heartland in the Ruhr, the Wehrmacht fortified the border area around Aachen with a double line of bunkers. The campaign in the autumn of 1944 and the winter of 1944/45 was one of the most frustrating and costly efforts by the US Army in the European theater in World War II, reaching its crescendo in the hellish fighting for the Hürtgen forest. Although the US Army finally broke through the defenses by the middle of December 1944 and reached the River Roer, the German counter-offensive in the neighboring Ardennes put a temporary halt to the fighting. It resumed in February 1945, culminating in Operation *Grenade*, the crossing of the Roer.

RIGHT **On September 13, 1944 Task Force X of the 3rd Armored Division penetrated the Siegfried Line near Aachen. Here, one of the division's M4 tanks drives through some dragon's teeth, the first layer of the Scharnhorst Line. (NARA)**

LEFT **A pair of GIs take cover from the incessant rain under the rear of an M4 tank. They are from 2/60th Infantry, 9th Division, which teamed up with Task Force Hogan of the 3rd Armored Division to assault the village of Geich beyond the Langerwehe industrial area on December 11, 1944. (NARA)**

CHRONOLOGY

1944

September 11	Reconnaissance patrol of the 5th Armored Division is the first to cross German border over the River Our.
September 12	3rd Armored Division begins probes of Scharnhorst Line of the Westwall near Aachen.
September 15	3rd Armored Division reaches Schill Line near Aachen.
September 17	12th Infantry Division arrives near Stolberg; first substantial German reinforcements of the campaign.
September 17	Operation *Market Garden* begins in the late afternoon in the neighboring 21st Army Group sector in the Netherlands.
September 22	Hodges orders temporary halt to offensive operations due to lack of supplies.
October 2	XIX Corps begins drive to breach Westwall north of Aachen.
October 8	VII Corps begins attempt to encircle Aachen and link with XIX Corps to the north.
October 10	US Army issues surrender ultimatum to Aachen garrison.
October 11	Bombardment of Aachen begins.
October 13	Infantry assault into Aachen by 26th Infantry begins.
October 16	Encirclement of Aachen completed at 1615 hours near Ravels Hill.
October 21	German forces in Aachen surrender at 1205 hours.
November 2	US 28th Division begins attack into the Hürtgen forest.
November 4	German counterattack retakes Schmidt.
November 6	US defense of Vossenack falters, but Germans capture only part of town.
November 7	German counterattack retakes Kommerscheidt; 28th Division withdraws from the Kall ravine.
November 16	Operation *Queen* begins with heavy air bombardment.
November 17	Major counterattack by 9th Panzer Division against advancing 2nd Armored Division.
November 20	Advance by the 4th Infantry Division in the Hürtgen is so slow that V Corps takes over and adds the 8th Infantry Division.
November 20	2nd Armored Division takes its major objective, Gereonsweiler.
November 21	Eschweiler is captured by the 104th Division.
November 28	The town of Hürtgen finally falls to the 8th Division.
November 29	Grosshau in the Hürtgenwald is finally captured by the 4th Division.
November 29	84th Division seizes Lindern.
December 2	Brandenberg in the Hürtgenwald is captured by the 5th Armored Division.
December 3	83rd Division replaces the battered 4th Division in the Hürtgen.
December 7	VII Corps calls a temporary halt to offensive; restarts on December 10.
December 16	Germans launch Operation *Wacht am Rhein*, the Ardennes offensive.

THE STRATEGIC SITUATION

By the middle of September 1944, the Wehrmacht in the west was in a desperate crisis. Following the Allied breakout from Normandy in late July, the German forces in northern France had become enveloped in a series of devastating encirclements starting with the Roncey pocket in late July, the Falaise pocket in mid August, the River Seine in late August, and the Mons pocket in Belgium in early September. The three weeks from August 21 to September 16 were later called the "void" by German commanders as the German defensive positions in northern France and Belgium disintegrated into rout and chaos in the face of onrushing Allied forces. These catastrophes destroyed much of the 7th and 15th armies along with parts of the 19th Army. On August 15, 1944, the US Army staged a second amphibious landing on the Mediterranean coast in southern France. The US Seventh Army raced northward towards Lorraine, threatening to cut off the remainder of German occupation forces in western and central France. As a result, there was a hasty withdrawal of the German 1st Army from the Atlantic coast as well as elements of the 19th Army from central France, precipitously ending the German occupation of

GIs warily peer around a corner in Thimister, Belgium on September 11, on the way to Aachen. (NARA)

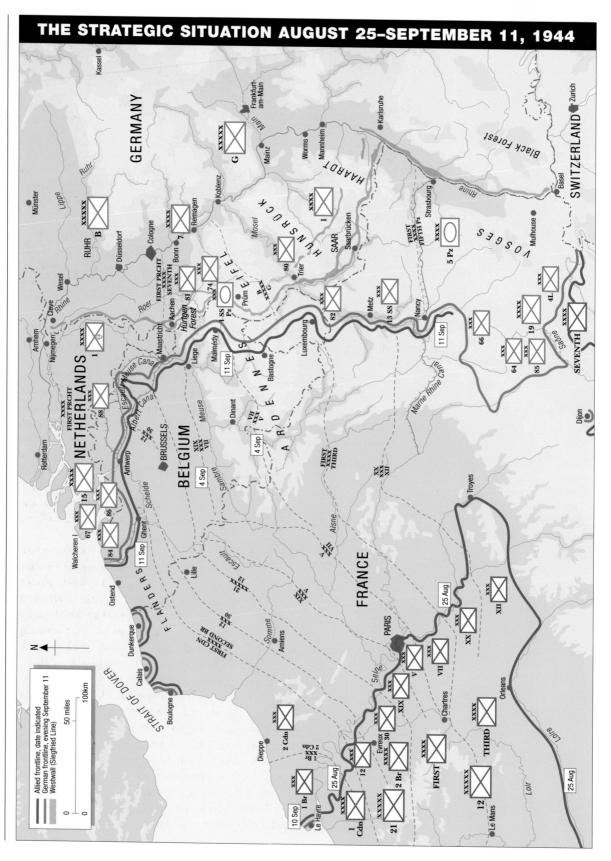

Since their construction in 1938–40, many of the Westwall bunkers had become abandoned and overgrown like this example near Aachen. (NARA)

France. German losses in the west in the late summer totaled over 300,000 troops, and another 200,000 were trapped in various ports along the Atlantic, such as Brest, Lorient, and Royan.

The situation on the Russian Front was even worse, with Army Group Center having been destroyed at the start of the Soviet summer offensive and the Wehrmacht pushed entirely out of the Soviet Union into Poland and the Balkans. Germany's eastern alliances collapsed as Finland and Romania switched sides, and in the process the vital Romanian oilfields were lost. The Red Army was already in East Prussia and had advanced as far as the Vistula before running out of steam in August. The Wehrmacht was on the brink of anarchy with commanders unable to halt their retreating troops, and new defense lines manned by inexperienced and untested soldiers. Casualties during the summer had totaled 1.2 million troops and a quarter million horses.

From the perspective of Gen Dwight Eisenhower's Supreme Headquarters-Allied Expeditionary Force (SHAEF), the strong feeling was that the Wehrmacht was in its death throes, much like the German Army on the Western Front in November 1918. German officers had tried to kill Hitler in July, and it seemed entirely possible that the Wehrmacht would totally collapse. After the stupendous advance of the past month, bold action seemed the order of the day. The otherwise cautious Gen Bernard Montgomery proposed an audacious and imaginative plan to streak through the Netherlands by seizing a bridge over the Rhine at Arnhem. This would propel the 21st Army Group into Germany's vital Ruhr industrial region, which would effectively cripple the German war industry. Operation *Market Garden*, a combined airborne-mechanized campaign from Eindhoven to Arnhem, proved to be a disappointing failure. Instead of facing a retreating rabble, the Wehrmacht seemed to grow in strength the closer the Allies approached the German frontier. By the third week of September, it was becoming clear that the Wehrmacht had already reached its nadir and was beginning to recover its ferocious defensive potential. This abrupt change was later dubbed the "miracle of the west."

The momentum of the campaign in northwest Europe began to slow abruptly in mid September as the Allies outran their supply lines. Initial planning had not anticipated that the Allied armies would advance so rapidly, and logistics were beginning to place a limit on Allied operations. On September 11, 1944, the first day US troops entered Germany, the Allies were along a phase line that the Operation *Overlord* plans did not expect to reach until D+330 (May 2, 1945) – some 233 days ahead of schedule. While Montgomery was attempting to reach the "bridge too far" at Arnhem, Patton's Third Army had been forced to halt in Lorraine, even though the path seemed open for a rapid advance on Frankfurt and the Rhine. Allied logistics could only support one major offensive at a time until new supply lines could be established. The rail network through France had been smashed by Allied pre-invasion bombing and many of the French ports had been thoroughly wrecked before the German garrisons had surrendered. Although the British army had seized the vital port of Antwerp largely intact, in the haste to reach the Rhine the vital issue of clearing the Scheldt estuary had been ignored. As a result, German forces could interdict shipping moving down the Scheldt to Antwerp, effectively blocking the port. Antwerp was the natural logistics center for further operations into Germany, and until the Scheldt could be cleared, Allied operations would have to operate on a thin stream of supplies. The failure to clear the approaches to Antwerp during the Wehrmacht retreat in early September proved to be one of the greatest Allied mistakes in 1944.

The German situation in the early autumn of 1944 was still desperate, but as the Wehrmacht reached the German frontier, the summer panic subsided and a sober stoicism returned. It was one thing to give up Holland and Belgium without a fight, but the western region of Germany was another matter altogether. By the time that the retreating survivors of Army Group B reached the frontier, new defenses had already been stitched together along the Siegfried Line using replacement units, local training units, and an assortment of rear-area troops. In open combat against Allied mechanized formations, such defenders stood little chance. But the German frontier was well suited to defense. The terrain was a mixture of industrial towns bisected by numerous rivers and interspersed with wooded forests and hills, such as the Reichswald and Hürtgenwald. The autumn of 1944 was unusually wet; almost double the usual quantity of rain fell. The mud dampened the chances for Allied mechanized operations and the overcast skies constrained air-support operations.

OPPOSING COMMANDERS

GERMAN COMMANDERS

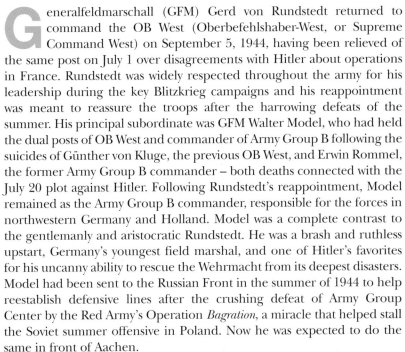

Generalfeldmarschall (GFM) Gerd von Rundstedt returned to command the OB West (Oberbefehlshaber-West, or Supreme Command West) on September 5, 1944, having been relieved of the same post on July 1 over disagreements with Hitler about operations in France. Rundstedt was widely respected throughout the army for his leadership during the key Blitzkrieg campaigns and his reappointment was meant to reassure the troops after the harrowing defeats of the summer. His principal subordinate was GFM Walter Model, who had held the dual posts of OB West and commander of Army Group B following the suicides of Günther von Kluge, the previous OB West, and Erwin Rommel, the former Army Group B commander – both deaths connected with the July 20 plot against Hitler. Following Rundstedt's reappointment, Model remained as the Army Group B commander, responsible for the forces in northwestern Germany and Holland. Model was a complete contrast to the gentlemanly and aristocratic Rundstedt. He was a brash and ruthless upstart, Germany's youngest field marshal, and one of Hitler's favorites for his uncanny ability to rescue the Wehrmacht from its deepest disasters. Model had been sent to the Russian Front in the summer of 1944 to help reestablish defensive lines after the crushing defeat of Army Group Center by the Red Army's Operation *Bagration*, a miracle that helped stall the Soviet summer offensive in Poland. Now he was expected to do the same in front of Aachen.

GFM Walter Model commanded Army Group B and he is seen here with Gen Maj Gerhard Engel, commander of the 12th Infantry Division. (MHI)

The Aachen corridor was defended by the 7th Army, commanded by Gen Erich Brandenberger. Model derided him as "a typical product of the general staff system" and his traditional style did not earn him the favor of Hitler. Yet Brandenberger had a fine combat record, leading the 8th Panzer Division during the invasion of Russia in 1941 and commanding the 29th Army Corps in Russia for a year before being given command of the 7th Army.

One of Brandenberger's initial tasks was to restore some measure of order amongst his edgy corps and divisional commanders. The "void" of late August and early September had left many divisional commanders to operate on their own initiative and it was Brandenberger's task to reestablish iron discipline. A good example of the confused temper of the time was the fate of the highly respected but headstrong commander of the 116th Panzer Division, Gen Lt Graf Gerhard von Schwerin. The young count already had a reputation for being more concerned about the fate of his troops than for instructions from higher headquarters, and during the abortive Panzer counteroffensive around Mortain in the summer, had been relieved for flaunting instructions on the disposition of his division. Following the Falaise debacle, he was reappointed

General der Panzertruppen Erich Brandenberger commanded the 7th Army through the Ardennes campaign. (MHI)

Gen Lt Graf Gerhard von Schwerin commanded the 116th Panzer Division during the initial defense of Aachen. (NARA)

commander, but, during the short-lived defense of Liège, he again frustrated the corps commanders by his independent actions. It was well known among the divisional officers that Schwerin did not want to continue fighting on German soil for fear of the desolation that would ensue. When Schwerin first took command of the Aachen defenses on September 12, he found that Nazi party leaders and police had already abandoned the city and that the civilian population was in chaos; he halted the exodus out of the city, not realizing that it had been Hitler who had ordered it. Hoping that the city would be abandoned rather than defended to the last, he left a message with a city official intended for the US Army asking them "to take care of the unfortunate population in a humane way." Unfortunately, on September 15 the Nazi party leaders and some police skulked back into the city and discovered the note. They accused Schwerin of defeatism and tried to haul him before a "People's Court." Schwerin ignored them and later in the month presented himself to Seventh Army headquarters for a military tribunal. Appreciating Schwerin's gallantry, Rundstedt proposed reinstating him to divisional command. However, in the paranoid climate around Hitler after the officers' bomb plot, he was sent for a while to the "doghouse" – the OKW officers' pool – until things cooled off. He later commanded a Panzergrenadier division and a corps in Italy. Brandenberger also relieved Gen Schack of command of 81st Corps on September 20 due to his connection with the Schwerin affair.

US COMMANDERS

At the beginning of September 1944, Bradley's 12th Army Group included two armies, Hodges' First and Patton's Third. Bradley had headed the First Army when it landed in Normandy, and was bumped upstairs once Patton's Third Army was activated in August 1944. Hodges had been Bradley's chief of staff in the First Army and succeeded him. Much like Bradley, Hodges was a quiet professional, and so very much unlike the flamboyant George S. Patton. However, Hodges did not have Bradley's intellectual talents and had flunked out of the US Military Academy, making his way up the command ladder through the ranks. He was in Bradley's shadow for much of the war, and many senior officers felt he gave too much power to his dynamic chief of staff, Maj Gen William Kean. Hodges was an infantryman with a dependable but stolid operational style.

At the time of the Aachen fighting, Hodges had three corps: Gerow's V Corps, Collins' VII Corps and Corlett's XIX Corps. Like Hodges, Maj Gen Leonard Gerow was older than both Bradley and Eisenhower, coming from the Virginia Military Institute class of 1911. He commanded Eisenhower in 1941 while heading the War Plans division of the general staff, and he led V Corps during the D-Day landings on Omaha Beach. He was a quintessential staff officer with a tendency to micromanage his divisional commanders, and so was a comfortable fit with the First Army commander. When Hodges needed more tactical flair, he turned to Maj Gen Lawton "Lightning Joe" Collins. He had commanded an army division on Guadalcanal in 1943, and had proven to be an imaginative practitioner of mechanized warfare in France. Collins had executed the

Lt Gen Courtney Hodges, commander of the US First Army. (NARA)

LEFT **Maj Gen Leonard Gerow, commander of V Corps. (NARA)**

RIGHT **Maj Gen Charles "Cowboy Pete" Corlett, commander of XIX Corps. (NARA)**

most impressive US Army successes of the summer, the envelopment of Cherbourg in June and the Operation *Cobra* breakout in July. Although he had a very different tactical sensibility to Hodges, they proved to be a complementary team through the war. The third corps commander, Maj Gen Charles "Cowboy Pete" Corlett was the odd man out in the First Army. He had commanded army units in the Aleutians in 1943 and on Kwajalein in 1944, and was brought to Europe in the hope that some of his amphibious experience would rub off on D-Day planners. He was widely ignored, and as a result, he had a chip on his shoulder over his continued lack of influence within First Army. For example, he had pointedly recommended increasing the artillery ammunition allowances based on his own experience, only to be proven right in the autumn when US Army ammunition reserves proved to be woefully inadequate. Corlett had several angry exchanges with Hodges and his staff, and was relieved during the Aachen campaign for "health reasons" – in fact this was due to his disputatious relations with Hodges. He had hardly arrived back in Washington for rest when he was bundled off to the Pacific again for another corps command, so high was his reputation in that theater.

First Army was blessed with an array of superior divisional commanders such as Huebner with the 1st Infantry, Harmon with the 2nd Armored, Rose in the 3rd Armored, Barton in the 4th Infantry, and many more. One of the divisional commanders was new, Norman Cota of the 28th Division. He had commanded the 116th Regimental Combat Team of the 29th Division on Omaha Beach on D-Day and his exceptional leadership that day earned him command of the 28th Division. The tragic fate of the 28th Division, first in the Hürtgen forest in October 1944 and then in the Ardennes in December, would haunt his career.

When Simpson's Ninth Army arrived in late September, Bradley placed it adjacent to the British 21st Army Group. Bradley was aware of Montgomery's tendency to poach US forces to make up for his own shortages, and he did not want his more experienced divisions in the First Army transferred to British control. Ninth Army was fairly small during the Aachen campaign, with only a single corps for much of the time.

Maj Gen Lawton "Lightning Joe" Collins, commander of VII Corps. (NARA)

OPPOSING ARMIES

THE WEHRMACHT

The complete collapse of the Wehrmacht after the disasters in Belgium in early September 1944 was partly averted by absorbing territorial and training units once its battered divisions reached Germany. The Wehrmacht consisted of both a Field Army, which controlled tactical combat units, and a separate Replacement Army (*Ersatzheer*) within Germany itself. In desperation, the untrained units from the reserve training divisions and sometimes even the staffs of the training schools were thrown into combat. Each military district also had several Landesschützen battalions for territorial defense, local home guard units made up of men "as old as the hills" armed with aging rifles, and usually commanded by World War I veterans.

Another source of personnel for the army was the Luftwaffe, since many of its ground personnel were freed from their usual assignments by the growing fuel shortage that grounded many aircraft in the autumn of 1944. While some men were absorbed directly into replacement units, others were organized into Luftwaffe fortress battalions. These battalions were not necessarily assigned to the Westwall bunkers; they were so named because their troops had little infantry training and were poorly armed, and so were useful only for holding static defense positions. These units were not well regarded by the army due to their tendency to retreat on first contact with enemy forces, and in subsequent months the army preferred to simply absorb excess Luftwaffe and navy personnel directly into army units.

Older men were swept into the army to make up for shortages. This old *Landser* was captured near the town of Hürtgen in early December 1944. (NARA)

The unification of command of these disparate units did not take place until early September, with the reconstitution of the 7th Army. Following the encirclement in the Falaise pocket and the deeper envelopment on the Seine, the German 7th Army ceased to exist and its remnants were attached to the 5th Panzer Army. On September 4, 1944, it was reconstructed under Gen Erich Brandenberger and assigned the task of defending the Westwall in the Maastricht–Aachen–Bitburg sector, with its 81st Corps covering from the Herzogenrath–Düren area, the 74th Corps from Roetgen to Ormont and the 1st SS-Panzer Corps in the Schnee Eifel from Ormont to the 1st Army boundary near Diekirch. The 81st Corps covered the sector attacked by the US VII and XIX Corps and most of its main combat elements were still withdrawing through Belgium into the second week of September. The 353rd Infantry Division had little more than its headquarter elements, so the 81st Corps used it to man the Westwall defenses in the Aachen area by assigning it the various Luftwaffe and Landesschützen battalions. The northern sector facing the US XIX Corps was held by two significantly understrength infantry divisions, the 49th and 275th. The 49th Infantry Division had been trapped in the Mons pocket, and by the time it reached the German frontier it had only about 1,500 men, mostly from the headquarters and support elements. The 275th Infantry Division suffered terribly in Normandy and by August it was described as "practically destroyed." It was partly rebuilt and by mid September had only one infantry regiment. It had a divisional strength of 5,000 men and a combat strength of about 1,800 men but its field artillery was limited to a single battery of 105mm howitzers.[1]

The principal units facing the US VII Corps were the 116th Panzer Division, centered around Aachen, and the 9th Panzer Division in the Stolberg corridor. The 116th Panzer Division was the best-equipped unit in this sector, but, when it took control of the defense of Aachen in mid September, it had a combat strength of about 1,600 men, with its Panzergrenadier battalions about half-strength and only three PzKpfw IV tanks, two Panther tanks, and two StuG III assault guns. Reinforcements in the third week of September reestablished its combat strength in infantry, but it was down to only about 2,000 liters (500 gallons) of fuel, leaving it immobilized. The 9th Panzer Division was still withdrawing through Belgium and was a mere skeleton. Its armored strength had been reduced to eight operational Panther tanks, and six StuG III assault guns; its two Panzergrenadier regiments were down to about three companies. The division was so weak that the 7th Army reinforced it with the remnants of Panzer Brigade 105, which had lost most of its Panzergrenadiers and was down to five Panther tanks and three assault guns. After the surviving battlegroup withdrew across the frontier, the division was rebuilt with a hodgepodge of territorial and Luftwaffe units in its sector.

Recognizing the weakness of the units assigned to the 81st Corps, the 7th Army attempted to reinforce the Aachen sector as soon as resources became available, and three divisions were assigned in mid September. The first to arrive was the 12th Infantry Division, which had been reconstituted in East Prussia in the late summer after heavy combat on the Russian Front.

---

1 The Wehrmacht defined combat strength as the number of frontline combat troops; it did not include non-combat elements, so, for example, a full-strength infantry division with 14,800 men had a combat strength of 3,800.

One of the most effective weapons in the autumn 1944 fighting was the PaK 40 75mm antitank gun, the standard weapon of German infantry divisions and frequently misidentified by US troops as an 88mm gun. This example was captured in the fighting near Aachen. (NARA)

Its arrival in the Aachen sector starting on September 14 was a major morale boost for the locale civilian population, as the division was fully equipped with young, new soldiers. The two other divisions were the 183rd and 246th Volksgrenadier divisions (VGD). The 183rd VGD arrived in the sector on September 22 and was assigned to take over the Geilenkirchen sector from the 275th Infantry Division, which was then shifted to cover a gap on the corps' southern wing in the Hürtgen forest. The 183rd VGD was moved from Bohemia starting on September 23. Its arrival permitted the 116th Panzer Division to be gradually pulled out of the line for refitting and to serve as the corps reserve.

7th Army	General der Panzertruppe
	Erich Brandenberger
81st Corps	**Generalleutnant Friederich-August Schack**
49th Infantry Division	Generalleutnant Siegfried Macholz
275th Infantry Division	Generalleutnant Hans Schmidt
116th Panzer Division	Generalleutnant Graf Gerhard von Schwerin
9th Panzer Division	Generalmajor Gerhard Müller
353rd Infantry Division	Generalleutnant Paul Mahlmann
Reinforcements after September 14	
12th Infantry Division	Colonel Gerhard Engel
183rd Volksgrenadier Division	Generalleutnant Wolfgang Lange

The Siegfried Line

The Westwall program began in 1938, but the role of the Westwall was fundamentally different from the much more elaborate Maginot Line nearby in France. It was intended as a defensive fortified zone facilitating offensive action. By 1938, Hitler was already planning military actions against Czechoslovakia and Poland, and fortifications played a vital part in these plans. The Westwall could be held by a modest number of second-rate troops while the bulk of the Wehrmacht was deployed in combat to the east. The initial construction program ignored the Aachen area, since it faced neutral Belgium. Once the section facing central

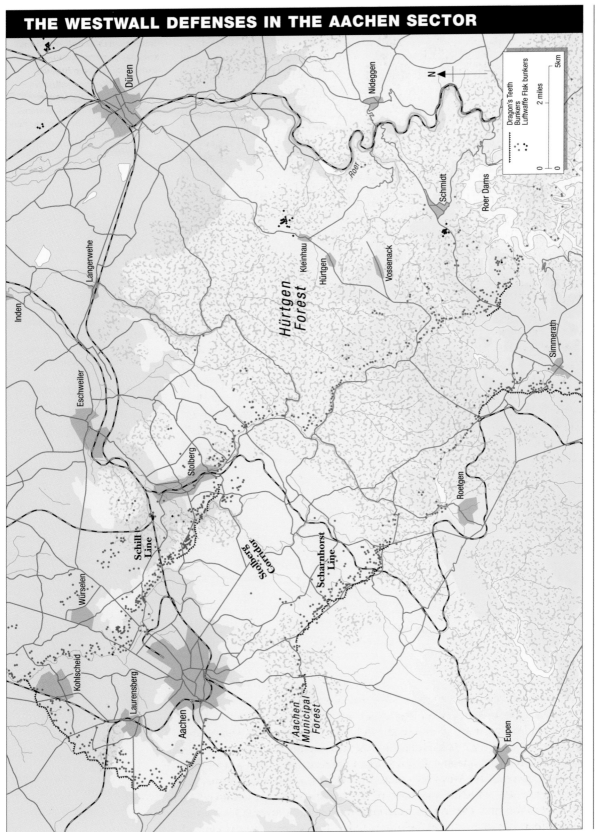

Düren

Nideggen

Roer

Schmidt

Roer Dams

Langerwehe

Kleinhau

Hürtgen

Vossenack

Hürtgen Forest

Inden

Simmerath

Eschweiler

Stolberg

Roetgen

Schill Line

Stolberg Corridor

Scharnhorst Line

Würselen

Kohlscheid

Laurensberg

Aachen

Aachen Municipal Forest

Eupen

Dragon's Teeth
Bunkers
Luftwaffe Flak bunkers

0   2 miles
0   5km

A typical stretch of the Westwall with rows of dragon's teeth in the background covered by an armored machine-gun position. These cupolas were the only visible portion of a much more extensive infantry bunker underneath. (NARA)

This armored machine-gun cupola from the Westwall near Wahlerscheid is typical of the type of defenses built in the forests along the German frontier, positioned to cover firebreaks and other access routes through the forest. (NARA)

France was complete, Hitler decided to extend the Westwall along the Belgian frontier due to concerns that the French could deploy their mobile forces through Belgium.

The Westwall in the Aachen area, called the Düren Fortification Sector (*Festungsdienststelle Düren*) was one of only two sectors with a double set of defensive lines. The other was in the Saar, which like the Aachen corridor was one of the traditional invasion routes between France and Germany. The initial defensive line was called the Scharnhorst Line and was located about a kilometer behind the German border. A second defensive belt, called the Schill Line, was created to the east of Aachen. The Westwall was a far less elaborate defensive system than the Maginot Line. With few exceptions, the fortifications were relatively small infantry bunkers with machine-gun armament, and few of

While many bunkers used natural camouflage, some were cleverly blended in with neighboring buildings, such as this bunker camouflaged to resemble an ordinary house in Steinfeld. (NARA)

By 1944, the Westwall bunkers had become overgrown and well camouflaged, like this one in the woods outside Aachen encountered by the 1st Infantry Division. (NARA)

the elaborate artillery bunkers that characterized the French defenses. There was never any expectation that the Westwall alone could hold out against a determined enemy, but after the experiences of trench warfare in World War I, there was a clear appreciation that modest fortifications could amplify the defensive capabilities of the infantry. The Westwall began with a barrier of antitank ditches and concrete dragon's teeth antitank obstacles. The layout and density of the subsequent bunkers depended on the geography and were designed to exploit local terrain features. Machine-gun bunkers were placed to cover all key roads and approaches as well as to prevent the antitank obstacles from being breached. Antitank bunkers were equipped with the 37mm antitank gun – adequate in 1939 but obsolete in 1944. Another characteristic type of bunker was a forward observation post for artillery spotters, connected to

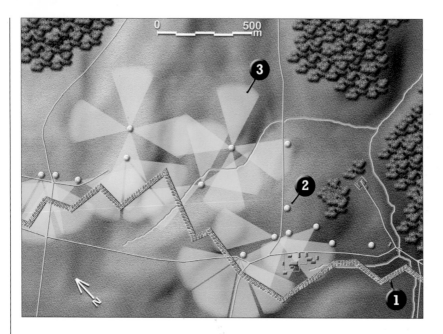

This schematic shows a typical stretch of the Westwall near Aachen in the area first penetrated by the 1/26th Infantry. The dragon's teeth (1) were positioned in front, with a string of bunkers behind (2); the bunker's machine guns provided overlapping fields of fire (3). (Author's illustration)

the rear to take maximum advantage of artillery firepower in defending the frontier. In the Aachen area, the Westwall had a linear density of about 60 bunkers per 10km stretch. Some idea of the relative distribution of the bunkers can be seen in the following table of the Düren Fortification Sector, which included the Aachen area.

Düren Fortification Sector

Type	Infantry	Antitank	Artillery	Total
Main belt	1,413	128	109	1,650
Other	814	123	138	1,075
Total	2,227	251	247	2,725
Accommodation	31,253	1,533	3,544	36,330

During 1943–44, the Westwall was stripped of anything removable such as wire obstructions, armored doors, gun mounts and armored fittings to equip the Atlantikwall against the impending Allied invasion. As a result, when the Wehrmacht retreated into Germany in September 1944 the Westwall was overgrown and largely abandoned. There was a hasty effort to refurbish the defenses in August–September 1944.

THE US ARMY

The US Army by the time of the Siegfried Line campaign had moved beyond its growing pains and had become an experienced and highly capable force. First Army included some of the most experienced US units in the ETO, such as the 1st Infantry Division and 2nd Armored Division, which had served in North Africa, Sicily, and Normandy; nearly all of the other divisions had been in combat since July. Combat leaders were experienced and battle hardened. For example, in a typical regiment – the 22nd Infantry of the 4th Division – officer casualties from D-Day to

One of the most effective weapons during the Siegfried Line campaign was the M12 155mm GMC, seen here during the fighting in the Hürtgenwald near Gürzenich on November 16. It was used for bunker busting along the Westwall, and also during the urban fighting, such as in Aachen. (NARA)

the start of the Hürtgen fighting in November had been 283 from an authorized strength of 152; 40 percent of its officers had been wounded and returned to service, and 12 of its lieutenants were battlefield commissions. It was a similar story in the enlisted ranks: the 22nd Infantry had suffered 4,329 casualties since D-Day out of an authorized strength of 3,100. The US Army had not yet begun to suffer the serious shortages in infantrymen caused by the autumn and winter 1944 fighting, so infantry divisions tended to operate near full strength. The US Army continued to feed replacements into the divisions in combat, and, while rifle companies were often understrength during intense battles, they seldom became as depleted as German rifle companies in 1944. US Army replacement policy has often been criticized as inefficient compared to the German system, but this traditional viewpoint has been seriously questioned by more recent scholarship on the subject.[2]

The US infantry divisions had adapted well to the changing terrain and tactical demands of the ETO, from the hedgerow country of Normandy in June and July, the pursuit operations of August, and the fortification and urban fighting of September–October. In contrast, the Hürtgen forest fighting proved to be especially costly and frustrating for the infantry. In many respects, the forest fighting was an aberration due to the lack of tactical flexibility at the lower levels forced on the infantry divisions by the orders of higher headquarters. The divisions fought on extended frontages in difficult weather and terrain conditions with little or no tank support, poor logistical support, and little opportunity to maneuver. Artillery was the main killer on both sides, and the US infantry was at a distinct disadvantage due to its offensive posture. Advancing American infantrymen were far more vulnerable to artillery

Anticipating the Siegfried Line, in September 1944 the First Army brought up flamethrowers to deal with the bunkers. (NARA)

2 Of special note is the recent study by Robert S. Rush, *Hell in the Hurtgen Forest* (University of Kansas, 2001), which takes a detailed look at the experience of one US infantry regiment and its corresponding German opponents in the November 1944 fighting.

GIs hold a defensive position in the Hürtgen forest on November 17. The M1 57mm antitank gun was the standard antitank gun in infantry divisions in 1944, with 18 in each infantry regiment. However, it was not particularly effective against the newer German tanks such as the Panther. (NARA)

air-bursting in the trees overhead than the defending German infantry in log-protected dugouts. As a corollary, the usual US advantage in divisional field artillery did not apply in the Hürtgen forest, in spite of US advantages in ammunition supply and fire direction because of the decreased lethality of US artillery when used against protected German infantry dugouts in heavily wooded areas.

The US armored divisions fought as combined-arms formations, amalgamating their tank, armored infantry, and armored field artillery battalions into three battlegroups called combat commands. Two of the divisions in the First Army, the 2nd and 3rd Armored divisions, were under the old 1942 tables of organization and so had six instead of the later 1943 pattern of three tank battalions. Although stronger in tanks than the other "light" armored divisions, the imbalance in tanks created a need for more infantry and it was the usual practice to attach infantry battalions from neighboring infantry divisions to the combat commands during operations. The standard US tank of this period was the M4 "Sherman" medium tank, mostly with a 75mm dual-purpose gun but with an increasing number of 76mm guns optimized for the antitank role. The M4 was the best tank in combat in 1943 in North Africa, but by 1944 its time had passed and it was inferior to the better German tanks, such as the Panther, in terms of firepower and armor protection. This disparity was not especially significant in the Siegfried Line fighting, since there were so few German tanks present. However, the M4 had only moderate armor, which did not offer adequate protection against the most common German antitank gun, the 75mm PaK 40, or against infantry Panzerfaust antitank rockets, which were the main tank killers in the autumn fighting.

The summer campaign had been costly to the US armored divisions in both men and equipment, and many of the divisions were ragged and exhausted after nearly three months of continual combat. Tank losses during the August pursuit were the highest experienced by the US Army in Europe up to that time and were only surpassed during the Battle of

In the miserable rain and mud of autumn, one of the most useful vehicles was the tracked M29 Weasel, seen here pulling a jeep out of the mud during the fighting in the Hürtgenwald in October 1944.

the Bulge. The US Army had underestimated the likely loss rate of tanks in combat based on the experience in North Africa and Italy and so had only allotted a monthly attrition reserve of 7 percent compared to the British reserve of 50 percent. As a result, US tank units in the autumn typically fought at about 80–85 percent of authorized strength until the newly established attrition factor of 15 percent caught up. Some units had higher than average losses, and so, for example, in mid September 1944 the 3rd Armored Division was fighting with about half of its authorized tank strength.

A more serious supply deficit was in artillery ammunition, which had been substantially underestimated and as a result there was a shortage through most of the autumn. However, these shortages should be put in perspective, as by German standards US equipment and ammunition usage was luxurious. The Germans estimated that the US Army fired more than double the artillery ammunition that they did; Panzer strength in the autumn of 1944 was seldom above half of authorized strength.

The sole combat arm where the US Army clearly enjoyed both technological and tactical superiority was in field artillery. US infantry divisions had three 105mm battalions, which could be tasked to support each of the three infantry regiments in the division, plus a 155mm howitzer battalion for general support. While the cannons were not that much better than their German counterparts, they were fully motorized, and ammunition supply tended to be more ample with some rare exceptions. US artillery fire direction was a trendsetter, using a fire direction center (FDC) at divisional and corps level, linked by excellent tactical radios to mass fires. This facilitated novel tactics such as time-on-target (TOT) where all the cannon in a division or corps were timed for their first projectiles to arrive in a concentrated "serenade" on a single target almost instantaneously, greatly amplifying the lethality of the barrage since the enemy had no time to take cover. US corps artillery tended to include heavier weapons, not only additional 155mm howitzer battalions but also long-range 155mm guns, 8in. howitzers, and even the occasional 240mm howitzer battalion.

One of the main advantages the US Army possessed in the summer 1944 campaign had been tactical air support. The US First Army and the Ninth Tactical Air Force had worked out successful command and control to permit extremely effective frontline support by fighter-bombers, which was especially useful for disrupting German logistical support. US tactical air support proved far less effective in the autumn of 1944 due to poor weather, which frequently hindered or prevented air operations.

First Army	**Lt Gen Courtney Hodges**
V Corps	**Maj Gen Leonard Gerow**
4th Infantry Division	Maj Gen Raymond Barton
28th Division	Maj Gen Norman Cota
5th Armored Division	Maj Gen Lunsford Oliver
VII Corps	**Maj Gen Lawton Collins**
1st Infantry Division	Maj Gen Clarence Huebner
9th Infantry Division	Maj Gen Louis Craig
3rd Armored Division	Maj Gen Maurice Rose
XIX Corps	**Maj Gen Charles Corlett**
30th Division	Maj Gen Leland Hobbs
2nd Armored Division	Maj Gen Ernest Harmon

OPPOSING PLANS

US PLANS

Allied planning for the defeat of Germany intended to "rapidly starve Germany of the means to continue the war," with an emphasis on the capture of the two industrial concentrations in western Germany, the Ruhr and the Saar basin. Of the two, the Ruhr industrial region was the more significant, and the loss of the Ruhr combined with the loss of the Low Countries would eliminate 65 percent of German steel production and 56 percent of its coal production.

Four traditional invasion routes into Germany were considered: the Flanders plains, the Mauberge–Liège–Aachen corridor to the north of the Ardennes, the Ardennes–Eifel, and the Metz–Kaiserlautern gap. The Flanders plains were far from ideal for mechanized warfare due to the numerous rivers and water obstacles. The Ardennes was also ruled out due to the hilly, forested terrain, and its equally forbidding terrain on the German and Luxembourg side, the forested Eifel region in Germany, and the mountainous terrain around Vianden in Luxembourg. Of the two remaining access routes, the Aachen corridor was a traditional invasion route and the most practical. Although the terrain had some significant congestion points due to its high degree of industrialization, it offered the most direct route to the Ruhr. The Kaiserlautern gap was also attractive, especially for access to the Saar; however, its access to the Ruhr was more difficult up along the narrow Rhine Valley. As a result of these assessments, the Aachen corridor was expected to be the preferred route for the Allied advance.

Overextended logistics limited Allied operational goals in the autumn of 1944. Summer expedients like the Red Ball Express truck network were reaching their limit, consuming more fuel than they delivered. Here a Red Ball Express fuel column is seen near Alençon, France on September 2. (NARA).

Original Allied planning assumed that this mission would be undertaken by the British/Canadian 21st Army Group under Gen Bernard L. Montgomery. In the event, this did not occur due to other developments. The V-weapons campaign against Britain in the late summer of 1944 prompted Churchill to urge Eisenhower to push forces further north along the coast to capture German launch sites, and this task fell to the 21st Army Group. Montgomery insisted that Eisenhower cover his flank with at least one US army, and as a result the First Army was directed further north than might otherwise have been the case, leaving Patton's Third Army the task of assaulting the Metz–Kaiserlautern gap on its own. Although there were expectations that Montgomery's 21st Army Group would eventually be reoriented away from the Flanders plain and back towards the Aachen corridor, the decision to stage Operation *Market Garden* in the Netherlands tended to fix this northern orientation.

The failure of *Market Garden* had several implications for Allied operations in the early autumn of 1944. In the short term, it drained the Allied forces of their limited reserve of supplies and precipitated a temporary logistics crisis. The long-term consequence of the *Market Garden* operation was that it distorted original Allied strategic planning for the campaign into Germany. The British/Canadian 21st Army Group was now tied down on an axis facing the less desirable Flanders plains, not the Aachen corridor as had been expected. Bradley's 12th Army Group was bifurcated by the Ardennes, with Hodges' First Army covering Montgomery's southern flank whilst being aimed at the Aachen corridor, while Patton's Third Army was further south in Lorraine aimed along the Metz–Kaiserlautern axis. As a result, the US First and newly arrived Ninth armies fought a campaign completely disconnected from Patton's operations in the Saar, and the northern element of Bradley's 12th Army Group now faced the Aachen corridor instead of the anticipated Metz–Kasierlautern axis.

One of Eisenhower's options was to conduct relatively modest operations along the German frontier until the logistics caught up; this was the option chosen by the Red Army, which had halted operations on its central front in August 1944 to build up for the final offensive into Germany. Eisenhower was not keen on this option, fearing it would permit the Germans to rebuild the Wehrmacht in relative peace, and result in a more formidable opponent when the offensive resumed. Instead, Eisenhower decided to conduct limited offensive operations, which would drain the Wehrmacht by attrition. Some senior US commanders, such as Bradley, believed that it might be possible to reach the Rhine in the autumn, a viewpoint that gradually succumbed to reality in the face of determined German defenses along the Westwall.

GERMAN PLANS

The short-term objective in the Wehrmacht in September 1944 was simply to survive after the devastating losses of the month before. This process was greatly aided by two factors: the returning morale of the German troops on reaching German soil, and the halt in the Red Army offensive in Poland. The panic and chaos in the units of Army Group B quickly subsided in mid September. Even if the Westwall was more

For the Wehrmacht, the most immediate mission was to restore the army after the "void" of late August and early September, when defenses in the west seemed to disintegrate. Relieved to have survived the summer battles, these young German soldiers surrendered near Abbeville in early September. (MHI)

symbolic than real, there was a sense that the frontier could and should be defended. The halt of the Red Army offensive along the River Vistula in August 1944 also freed up resources for the western front. While fighting continued in the Balkans and in other peripheral theaters, the main front facing central Germany remained quiet until January 1945. The Wehrmacht was living on borrowed time. The loss of Romania's oilfields in the summer of 1944 doomed the German war effort, since it meant that petroleum would eventually run out. Although large coal reserves kept German industry running, fuel shortages led to a severe curtailment of Luftwaffe operations, cut training of Panzer and aircrews to a minimum, and led to severe restrictions on fuel usage, even in the combat theaters.

The central element in determining the shape of German operational planning in the west was Hitler's decision in September 1944 to launch a counteroffensive against the Allies sometime in the late autumn or early winter. The plan was dubbed *Wacht am Rhein* ("Watch on the Rhine"), a deliberate deception to suggest that the forces being mustered for the Ardennes attack were merely being gathered to conduct the eventual defense of the River Rhine. The first draft of the plan was completed on October 11 but it remained a secret to all but the most senior commanders such as Rundstedt and Model, who were briefed on October 22. The plan required that the most capable units, the Panzer, Panzergrenadier and best infantry divisions, be withheld from the autumn

The Nazi Party tried to assert discipline as the Allied armies approached German soil. This propaganda warning was painted on a wall in Aachen: "The enemy listens!" (NARA)

fighting and built back up to strength in time for the operation. Holding the River Roer was absolutely essential to the success of the Ardennes offensive, since, if the US Army advanced across the river, they could strike southward against the right flank of the attacking German forces. The challenge to Rundstedt and Model was to hold the River Roer line with an absolute minimum of forces while building up the strategic reserve for the Ardennes operation. This inevitably meant that the defense along the Roer would be conducted mainly by second-rate divisions that could be reinforced with fresher or more capable divisions only under the most dire circumstances. In their favor was the weather and geography. The autumn weather in 1944 was unusually rainy and the resultant mud made mechanized operations along the German frontier extremely difficult. In addition, it substantially suppressed the Allies' greatest advantage – their tactical air power. Geography aided the defense in two respects. On the one hand, the proximity of the front to German industry and supply dumps simplified German logistics, just as it complicated Allied logistics. On the other hand, the congested industrialized terrain of the Roer, and the mountainous forests of the Hürtgenwald, were well suited to defense.

THE CAMPAIGN

THE FIRST BATTLE OF AACHEN

The first US troops to reach German soil were a reconnaissance patrol of the 5th Armored Division, which crossed the River Our near Stalzemburg on the German–Luxembourg border on September 11, 1944. Although the V Corps made several other penetrations, on September 17 Gen Gerow halted any further attacks in this sector, realizing that his forces were too limited to conduct any deep penetration of the defenses in the wooded, mountainous terrain of the Eifel. After a few brief days of fighting, the Ardennes–Eifel front turned quiet, and would remain so for three months until the start of the German Ardennes offensive in this area on December 16.

Collins' VII Corps was moving on a 35-mile-wide front towards the Aachen corridor and began battalion-sized reconnaissance probes against the Scharnhorst Line of the Westwall on September 12. Aachen had been Charlemagne's capital and the imperial city of the kings of Germania from 936 to 1531; as a result Hitler was adamant that the city be defended. On September 16, Hitler issued a Führer directive. There was no room for strategic maneuver now that the enemy had reached German soil: every man was to "stand fast or die at his post." To facilitate the defense, Hitler ordered the civilians evacuated and by mid September, the population had fallen from 165,000 to about 20,000.

Engineers of the 3rd Armored Division plant demolition charges on dragon's teeth along the Scharnhorst Line in September, trying to blast another corridor towards Aachen. (NARA)

GIs of the 39th Infantry, 9th Infantry Division, riding on supporting M4 tanks of the 746th Tank Battalion, pass through the line of dragon's teeth of the Scharnhorst Line during the advance on Lammersdorf on September 15. (NARA)

The German 81st Corps assumed that the main US objective would be the city, and so assigned the defense to its best unit, the 116th Panzer Division, which began arriving on September 12.

In fact, the main objective of the VII Corps was to push up the Stolberg corridor with the aim of reaching the River Roer. The Combat Command B (CCB) of the 3rd Armored Division began moving forward at dawn on September 13, gradually battering its way up the Stolberg corridor. Closest to the city, the 16th Infantry stalled along the Westwall in the Aachen municipal forest. The penetrations accelerated over the next few days. The 1st Infantry Division pushed through the bunkers in the Aachen municipal forest, with two of its regiments reaching the southern outskirts of the city, while the 16th Infantry furthest east reached Ellendorf at the edge of the Schill Line. CCA of the 3rd Armored Division had the most dramatic gains, pushing all the way to the southern edge of Eilendorf to await infantry reinforcements. CCB of the 3rd Armored Division pushed northward out of the Monschau forest advancing with one task force into Kornelimunster and the other to the outskirts of Vicht. German resistance varied considerably; some of the Landesschütz territorial defense battalions evaporated on contact, while small rearguards from regular army units fought tenaciously. On September 15, both combat commands of the 3rd Armored Division penetrated into the Schill Line, with CCA coming under determined fire from StuG III assault guns holding the high ground near Geisberg, while the CCB's lead task force was stopped by tank fire from Hill 238 west of Gressenich. The 9th Panzer Division claimed the destruction of 42 US tanks that day – an exaggeration, but also a clear indication of the intensity of the fighting.

With the attack up the Stolberg corridor proceeding well, the 9th Infantry Division began a methodical advance into the Hürtgen forest on the right flank of the 3rd Armored Division, moving through both the Scharnhorst and Schill lines as far north as Schevenhütte. The attempt to clear the Hürtgen forest gradually ground to a halt after encountering elements of the 89th Infantry Division in bunkers of the Schill Line.

One tactic for dealing with Westwall bunkers was to blow open the rear door with a bazooka, as demonstrated by this team from the 24th Cavalry Reconaissance Squadron of the 4th Cavalry Group. (NARA)

The 9th Infantry Division reached Schevenhütte before being counterattacked by the newly arrived German 12th Infantry Division on September 17. A task force of the 3rd Armored Division intervened, and a pair of their M4A1 (76mm) tanks are seen in front of St Josef church on September 22. (NARA)

Even though the German defenders were outnumbered, the well-placed bunkers considerably amplified their combat effectiveness. The determined defense by the regular infantry was a complete contrast to earlier fighting against the initial Scharnhorst Line where local territorial defense units were not so resolute.

By now Gen Schack of the 81st Corps realized that the main US goal was to push through the Stolberg corridor, but the presence of the 1st Infantry Division on the doorstep of Aachen and the constant American shelling of the city suggested that the capture of the city was also an American objective. As a result, he kept Schwerin's 116th Panzer Division defending the city instead of attacking the flank of the American assault. The momentum of the battle shifted on September 17 following the arrival of the 12th VGD. This fresh, full-strength division had been allotted by Hitler to ensure the defense of Aachen, and was commanded

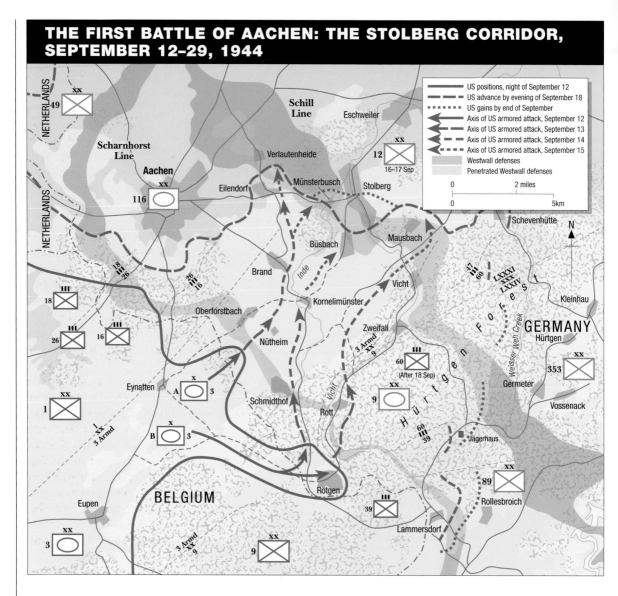

by one of Hitler's former military adjutants, Col Engel. Although Schack attempted to keep it intact for a decisive action, he was forced to commit it piecemeal, and an initial Fusilier Regiment 27 counterattack was beaten back with heavy losses. The arrival of these critical reinforcements permitted counterattacks all along the American lines, including determined attacks against the US 9th Infantry Division near Schevenhütte by Grenadier Regiment (GR) 48. With his own troops overextended and short of ammunition, Collins ordered his troops to consolidate their positions on the evening of September 17, except for the 9th Infantry Division still fighting in the Hürtgen. Skirmishes continued over the next few days with little movement as both sides tried to wrest control of key geographic features, such as the hills around Stolberg, and the towns of Verlautenheide and Schevenhütte. The Wehrmacht succeeded in halting the advance, but at a heavy cost in infantry. The newly arrived 12th VGD dropped in combat strength from 3,800 to 1,900 riflemen, and the 9th Panzer Division and its attachments lost over a thousand men, equivalent to about two-thirds of their combat strength compared to a week earlier.

Collins hoped that the 9th Infantry Division could push southeast out of the Hürtgen forest and seize the towns in the clearing on the road to Düren. With the fighting along the Stolberg corridor stalemated, the continuing US advance in the woods attracted the attention of the Seventh Army commander, Gen Brandenberger, who scraped up a few assault guns to reinforce the patchwork 353rd Infantry Division holding these towns. Both sides were badly overextended and exhausted, and small advantages could have a disproportionate effect. After repeated attempts, the 9th Infantry Division's push east through the wooded hills was halted short of the Hürtgen-Kleinhau clearings, ending the first attempt to clear the Hürtgen forest.

While most of the fighting by the US First Army had been concentrated in the VII Corps sector, Corlett's XIX Corps had taken advantage of the weak German defenses in the southern Netherlands to push up to the Westwall. In spite of the severe fuel shortages, the 2nd Armored Division pushed beyond the Albert Canal to Geilenkirchen, while on its right flank the 30th Division pushed towards Rimburg, an advance of some 15 to 33 miles in ten days. Nevertheless, German resistance was continuing to harden, and the XIX Corps was unable to intervene in the fighting around Aachen as a result.

With the launch of Operation *Market Garden* further north in the Netherlands by the 21st Army Group on September 17, US operations against the Westwall came to a halt for the rest of September. Low on supplies, out of fuel, overextended by the vagaries of the summer advance, and now facing a much more vigorous defense, it was time to recuperate and take stock. On September 22, Gen Hodges made this official, with instructions to shut down the remaining offensive operations in the VII Corps and XIX Corps sectors. During the final week of September, the US forces in the Aachen sector reorganized with the arrival of the Ninth Army. The new army was wedged between the British 21st Army Group to the north in the Netherlands, and the US First Army around Aachen.

NORTH OF AACHEN

To push to the River Roer, XIX Corps needed to breach the Westwall north of Aachen to come in line with VII Corps. By now, the Wehrmacht was alerted to the threat, and Gen Corlett expected the defenses to be fully prepared, unlike the situation in September. As a result, an effort was made to breach the Scharnhorst Line more methodically. In preparation, the XIX Corps artillery set about trying to eliminate as many bunkers as possible. It was evident from captured bunkers that the divisional 105mm and 155mm howitzers were not powerful enough to penetrate them. Fortunately, the US Army-ETO earlier in 1944 had anticipated the need for special weapons to deal with the Siegfried Line and had requested the dispatch of about seventy-five M12 155mm gun motor carriages to France. These were old World War I French 155mm GPF guns mounted on an M4 tank chassis, and they made formidable bunker-busters. The XIX Corps began a concerted campaign to bombard the German bunkers with

Once the 30th Division had penetrated the Westwall near Palenberg, the 2nd Armored Division exploited the breach and pushed on through Ubach. Here, an M4 tank of the 3/67th Armored takes up defensive positions outside the town on October 10. Having fought through the Siegfried Line, the front turned into a stalemate by early October.

divisional artillery to damage nearby field entrenchments and strip away camouflage from the bunkers. The M12 155mm GMC were then moved up close to the front under the cover of darkness, and set about attacking the bunkers from a few hundred yards away.

While the artillery preparations were under way, the infantry from the 30th Division was being trained in bunker-busting tactics. Two specialized weapons were issued: man-portable flamethrowers, and demolition charges mounted on poles to attack the vulnerable embrasures. Supporting tank units were also trained in bunker tactics, with some tanks being fitted with flamethrowers in place of the hull machine gun.

The attack by two regiments of the 30th Division against Rimburg–Palenberg was accompanied by feints further north and south to confuse the Germans as to the actual focal point. In the event, the new German 81st Corps commander, Gen Köchling, mistakenly believed that the renewed American offensive would again take place in the Stolberg corridor, and he viewed the preparations north of Aachen as a feint. The XIX Corps attack was preceded by a major air attack by medium bombers of the Ninth Air Force, but the October 2 bombing had little effect on German fortifications already ravaged by artillery over the past week. The first obstacle facing the 117th and 119th Infantry was the River Wurm, but they found that it was far less formidable than feared.

In the 117th Infantry sector, the new bunker-busting tactics proved very effective. Once artillery fire lifted, the embrasures were kept under machine-gun and bazooka fire while the infantry with pole-charges and flamethrowers advanced into range. The flamethrowers kept the pillboxes suppressed while the pole-charges were put into place against the embrasures or doors. Palenberg and Marienberg were captured by the end of the day, but the 119th Infantry was stalled by a disguised bunker reinforced by strongpoints near the medieval Rimburg castle. The next day, the 117th Infantry pushed into Ubach, but the 119th Infantry again became stalled after encircling and clearing the Rimburg castle. The capture of Ubach prompted Gen Corlett to commit a combat command of the 2nd Armored Division into the bridgehead earlier than expected in spite of the congestion.

The scale of the fighting on October 3 made it clear to Köchling that the focus of the attack was in the Palenberg–Rimburg sector, but reinforcements were slow in arriving and the planned counteroffensive in the early morning hours of October 4 fizzled out. The main attack emerged at dawn and managed to push back one US infantry company of the 119th Infantry before German artillery accidentally hit its own advancing troops, disrupting the attack. A third attack later in the day against Ubach ran into a planned attack by a task force of CCB, 2nd Armored Division, and the German infantry battalion was badly mauled. The other task force set out in the late afternoon under heavy German artillery fire, but once it exited Ubach, it picked up momentum. The locations of the German bunkers were well known, and coordinated tank-infantry attacks cleared them out. By nightfall, CCB had made some significant advances, though at a heavy cost in infantry and tanks. The American attacks had proven so worrisome that both Rundstedt and Brandenberger personally visited the 81st Corps headquarters and pledged to send Köchling as many reinforcements as they could muster to stamp out the American bridgehead.

In reality, German resources were stretched thin, and the reinforcements from the Seventh Army were the usual mishmash: NCO training school battalions from Düren and Jülich, a single battalion from the 275th Division, a fortress machine-gun battalion, and elements of an artillery brigade. Köchling himself was able to rearrange his corps in order to squeeze out a few more battalions for a counterattack. The October 5 counterattack was delayed by the usual problems of moving the troops into place, and many of the reinforcements were committed piecemeal to resist the renewed US attacks. German artillery fire proved to be unusually heavy, as Köchling had managed to shift more and more batteries into the threatened sector. By this stage, the German artillery included two railroad guns, a heavy howitzer battalion, forty-seven 150mm gun-howitzers, forty 105mm howitzers, thirty-two 88mm guns, and a variety of small-caliber

Troops of the 172nd Engineer Combat Battalion inspect German prisoners on October 6, following the capture of Ubach by the 2nd Armored Division. (NARA)

AACHEN STREET FIGHTING, OCTOBER 15, 1944
(pages 38–39)

In preparation for the attack into the center of Aachen, the 2/26th Infantry received specialized urban assault training developed on the spot by its commander, Lt Col Derrill Daniel. Short of manpower, Daniel was intent on substituting firepower for manpower and he dubbed the tactics as "knock'em all down." Each rifle company was organized as a task force with an attachment of three M4 medium tanks (1) or M10 tank destroyers (2), two 57mm antitank guns, two bazooka teams, a flamethrower, and two heavy machine-gun teams. To ensure that ammunition continued to flow in and casualties flowed out in a timely fashion, Daniel obtained M29 Weasel cargo carriers to deal with the rubble-filled streets. The tactics were to use firepower to chase the defenders into the cellars, at which point they would be attacked with grenades and flamethrowers. The attack was staged to systematically rout out the German defenders a street at a time, as seen here. The infantry would move along the sides of the street, using the buildings for cover, while the tanks and tank destroyers would move forward to provide direct firepower support. Co-ordination was

essential, and the German infantry was armed with the potent Panzerfaust antitank rocket. The task of the US infantry was to keep the German infantry at bay, so that they could not use the short-range Panzerfaust effectively. At least one M12 155mm GMC was used during the city fighting to knock out especially stubborn resistance points. Its 155mm gun could often bring down an entire building with only a few high-explosive rounds. By the time of the October 1944 fighting, the city had already been devastated by previous bombing and shelling. However, the streets were relatively clear of rubble, as the city government had attempted to keep main thoroughfares open until the evacuation on October 12. German defenses were based in the ruined housing and buildings, which offered a measure of protection against small-arms fire. However, the entire city garrison comprised only about 5,000 troops, and included a large number of Luftwaffe and naval personnel hastily transferred to the army in September with little or no infantry training. As a result, the two US attack battalions, although significantly outnumbered, were able to steadily advance and capture the city in less than a week.

weapons. The counterattack finally began on October 6 but was a pale shadow of the intended attack and the five assault-gun formations had been reduced to 27 vehicles. The American front exploded on October 7 when CCA, 2nd Armored Division moved into the breach. The 117th Infantry, with the support of the 743rd Tank Battalion, overran the German 49th Division, which by that stage had been reduced to a single infantry regiment. The advance put the 30th Division in Alsdorf, to the northeast of Aachen.

ENCIRCLING AACHEN

In less than a week, XIX Corps had punched a considerable hole in the Westwall north of Aachen and threatened to link up with VII Corps somewhere north of Stolberg. Kochling's 81st Corps at the time had four understrength divisions including the 49th and 183rd divisions that had been battered in the Palenberg–Rimburg fighting. The 246th VGD replaced the 116th Panzer Division in Aachen to permit its refitting, and the 12th Infantry Division was still in position southeast of Aachen to block any further advances by VII Corps. The effective combat strength of these four divisions was in the order of 18,000 infantry. Although German effective strength had fallen due to the fighting, its artillery had continued to increase and totaled 239 weapons, including one hundred and forty 105mm, eighty-four 150mm, and 15 heavy guns. Armored support was very weak compared with American strength, with only 12 serviceable StuG III assault guns; schwere Panzer Abteilung (s.Pz.Abt.) 508 had four Kingtiger tanks and Panzer Brigade 106 was down to seven Panthers. The Panzer units that had played such a central role in the fighting for the Stolberg corridor – the 9th and 116th Panzer Divisions and Panzer Brigade 105 – were refitting. To preempt the link-up of the American XIX and VII Corps, Model proposed launching a strong counteroffensive using the partly

On October 8, Mobile Regiment von Fritzchen attempted to push the 30th Division out of Alsdorf. Here the 117th Infantry has established an antitank defense in the streets of neighboring Schauffenburg using an M5 3in. antitank gun of the attached 823rd Tank Destroyer Battalion, along with a bazooka team and a .50-cal heavy machine gun. (NARA)

While Aachen was being encircled, 9th Division remained engaged in its efforts to push through the Hürtgen forest. Here, a 105mm M3 howitzer from a regimental cannon company is seen providing fire support on October 8.

reequipped 116th Panzer Division and 3rd Panzergrenadier Division (PGD) through the open terrain northeast of Aachen towards Jülich.

The US First Army planned to close the gap around Aachen using the overstretched 1st Infantry Division. The division was already deployed in a cordon defense around the southern edges of Aachen with only one regiment free for the assault, the 18th Infantry. The attack started in predawn hours of October 8, using combined tank-infantry tactics to bust open the bunkers in the Schill Line defenses. The initial objectives were a series of hills with commanding views of the area north of the city at Verlautenheide, Crucifix Hill and Ravels Hill. All three were captured by October 10. The main impediment to the American attack was the intense German artillery fire.

The XIX Corps attack from the north was conducted by the 30th Division aimed at Würselen. Against this advance, Model committed Mobile Regiment von Fritzchen – slapped together from three infantry battalions, and supported by 11 tanks of Panzer Brigade 108, a few Kingtigers from s.Pz.Abt 506 and 22 StuG III assault guns from three assault gun battalions. This battlegroup was ordered to clear Alsdorf of the 30th Division as a means of keeping open the corridor to Aachen. The initial advance by the 30th Division on October 8 went smoothly, but in mid morning the lead elements of 117th Infantry were struck on their eastern flank by elements of Mobile Regiment von Fritzchen from Mariadorf. This was only a part of the German attack, the other force attacking Alsdorf directly. The attack on Alsdorf found the town occupied by headquarters elements of the 117th Infantry, who set up a hasty defense. They were soon supported by some tanks of the 743rd Tank Battalion, which knocked out the four Panzers supporting the German infantry and helped to break the back of the attack. Although both attacks by Mobile Regiment von Fritzchen were beaten off with heavy German casualties, the 30th Division attack towards Würselen was halted for the day.

Mobile Regiment von Fritzchen was then shifted into the gap between the US 30th and 1st Infantry divisions in an attempt to prevent the link up. However, the German attacks on October 9 were frustrated by corresponding US attacks, and the 119th Infantry managed to push into northern Würselen by nightfall, only 2,000 yards from the 18th Infantry positions on Ravels Hill. This spearhead was hit that night by an attack of 300 infantry and five tanks from Panzer Brigade 108 around Bardenburg, which threatened the 30th Division advance. The capture of Birk the following morning by the 120th Infantry trapped the German force, but a fruitless day of fighting ensued with heavy casualties on both sides. On October 11, the 30th Division sent in its reserve, a single battalion of the 102nd Infantry, to finally wrest control of the town after it had been pummeled by artillery. Panzer Brigade 108's defenses had been stiffened by a battalion of half-tracks with quad 20mm anti-aircraft guns, but all six Panzers and 16 half-tracks were knocked out or captured, most falling victim to close-range bazooka attack.

The next elements of Model's counterattack force, arriving on October 11, included Kampfgruppe Diefenthal, which had been scraped together from survivors of the 1st and 12th SS-Panzer divisions, as well as Panzergrenadier Regiment (PGR) 60 of the 116th Panzer Division. In view of the gravity of the situation around Würselen, Model authorized Brandenberger to use the units as they became available instead of waiting for the whole force to arrive. As a result, the outlying positions of the 30th Division were hit by a succession of German attacks on October 12, heavily supported by Panzers. After days of overcast conditions, the weather that day was crystal clear, allowing Allied air power to intervene. The final push was reinforced by two battalions from the 116th Infantry, 29th Division, a battalion of tanks from the 2nd Armored Division, and an engineer battalion staging a direct frontal assault through the streets of Würselen. The attack was very slow going, since the town was occupied by the entire PGR 60, supported by dug-in Panzers, and little progress was made in three days of fighting.

Having already committed bits of the arriving 116th Panzer Division, Brandenberger received permission from Model to commit the 3rd PGD against the other wing of the American advance, the 18th Infantry positions on the hills around Verlautenheide. On the morning of October 14, PGR 29 supported by Kingtigers and captured M4 tanks of s.Pz.Abt. 506 attacked, but the opposing VII Corps artillery was waiting. When the attack formed up in the meadows in front of the US positions, it was hit by fire from six US artillery battalions, leading the divisional commander, Gen Maj Walter Dekert, to conclude that "it was obvious that an advance through this fire was impossible." The artillery stripped away the Panzergrenadiers, but a few Kingtiger tanks ploughed into the American lines and began shooting up the forward trenches. Panzergrenadier Regiment 8 tried to attack later, but was pummeled by artillery and subsequently strafed by a squadron of P-47 fighter-bombers. The violent attacks finally petered out by evening, with the US infantry still in control of their defenses. The 3rd PGD returned to the attack in the pre-dawn hours of October 15, nearly overrunning an infantry company in the dark. The US infantry huddled in their foxholes while US mortar fire and artillery landed nearly on top of them. As dawn arrived, the German survivors retreated into the early morning haze.

Fighting continued over the next few days, but on a much smaller scale. The 1st Division suffered 540 casualties in the three days of fighting, but the 3rd PGD lost a third of its effective strength.

With the German counteroffensive petering out, Hodges put more and more pressure on the 30th Division to finish the task by sealing the gap with the 1st Division. Since Würselen had proven impossible to take, Hobbs redirected the focus of the October 16 attack by the 119th Infantry west through Kohlscheid, while diversionary attacks were staged further east by the 117th and 120th Infantry. The diversions were costly, but managed to distract German artillery enough for the 2/119th Infantry to finally reach Hill 194 by late afternoon, within a thousand yards of the 1st Division positions. At 1615 hours, patrols from both divisions linked up near Ravels Hill, finally closing the Aachen gap.

THE SECOND BATTLE OF AACHEN

On October 10, the US Army sent a delegation into Aachen with a surrender ultimatum; based on Hitler's orders, it was rejected. Defending Aachen under the command of Col Gerhard Wilck was the 246th Division, which had three infantry battalions, two fortress battalions, some Luftwaffe troops, and about 125 city policemen. While understrength, Wilck's force actually outnumbered the attacking US infantry force about three to one. The 1st Infantry Division was so tied down defending the northern salient against attack that only two battalions of the 26th Infantry could be spared to assault the city center. The 2/26th Infantry was assigned the task of clearing the center of the old city while 3/26th Infantry took on the northern sector, which had a mixture of industrial, park and urban areas.

The reduction of the city began on October 11–12 with artillery and air attacks. The 1106th Engineer Group attempted to demolish buildings near the outskirts by filling trolley cars with captured explosives and then rolling them into the city. Although three of these "V-13's" were

The tactics of the 26th Infantry during the Aachen street fighting was to use firepower to reduce German defenses. Here, infantrymen of 2/26th Infantry look on while an M4 medium tank of the 745th Tank Battalion blasts away on October 15. (NARA)

A 57mm antitank gun fires on German defenses during the advance by Company E, 2/26th Infantry on October 15 in Aachen. (NARA)

German prisoners are escorted out of the city center by troops of the 2/26th Infantry on October 15. (NARA)

launched, they had little effect. The infantry assault began on the morning of October 13. Both battalions methodically pushed forward, clearing the area of both troops and a large number of German civilians still trapped in the basements. During the fighting, SS-Battalion "Rink" was sent into Aachen to reinforce the 246th Division, and Wilck assigned it the task of stopping the 3/26th Infantry advance. On October 15, 2/26th Infantry linked up with 3/26th Infantry and managed to secure a massive above-ground air-raid shelter that was housing about 200 soldiers and 1,000 civilians. With the two American columns closing in on the divisional headquarters at Hotel Quellenhof, Wilck ordered a counter-attack on the afternoon of October 15. The fighting along Hindenberg

GERMAN UNITS

12th SS Corps (as of October 17)
A 183rd Infantry Division

81st Corps
B 49th Infantry Division
C 46th Infantry Division
D 246th Infantry Division
E 12th Infantry Division

1st SS-Panzer Corps
F Mobile Group von Fritzchen
G Panzer Brigade 108
H Kampfgruppe Diefenthal
I Panzergrenadier Regiment 60 (116th Panzer Division)
J 3rd Panzergrenadier Division

GERMAN LINE, NIGHT OF OCTOBER 20

GERMAN LINE, MORNING OF OCTOBER 20

GEILENKIRCHEN

ALSDORF

KERKRADE

BARDENBURG

WESTWALL

▼ EVENTS

1. At dawn on October 8, the 18th Infantry spearheads the VII Corps assault to encircle Aachen, pushing through the 46th Infantry Division positions east of the city.

2. The 30th Division begins the XIX Corps assault in the pre-dawn hours of October 8, pushing southward against the 49th Infantry Division.

3. Model orders Mobile Group von Fritzchen to cut off 30th Division's attack; heavy fighting ensues when the Germans encounter the HQ of the 117th Infantry in Alsdorf. The Germans are eventually forced out.

4. The 119th Infantry reaches the fringe of Würselen by nightfall of October 9.

5. The 18th Infantry reaches Ravels Hill south of Würselen on October 9.

6. Late on October 9, remnants of Mobile Group von Frtizchen, mainly from Panzer Brigade 108, try to cut off the 30th Division spearheads near Bardenberg, and a two-day fight with the 120th Infantry ensues.

7. Model orders Kampfgruppe Diefenthal to begin an attack against US 1st and 30th Division spearheads around Würselen on October 12; PGR 60 takes up the defense of Würselen.

8. US attacks into Würselen take three days, even after a battalion of tanks from 2nd Armored Division arrives.

9. The 26th Infantry assault begins an attack on two axis into Aachen on the morning of October 13.

10. The 3rd PGD begins attacking 18th Infantry positions on Ravels Hill on October 14, with the fighting continuing for three days.

11. On October 15, the Aachen commander launches a counterattack by the 246th Division against the 2/26th Infantry along Hindenberg Strasse, and by SS-Battalion Rink against the 3/26th Infantry near Hotel Quellenhof.

12. The 30th Division switches its emphasis of attack away from Würselen, and, following feints by the 116th and 120th Infantry regiments, the 119th Infantry manages to link up near Ravels Hill at 1615 hours, October 16. Fighting to secure the Aachen corridor continues for several days.

13. Col Wilck and the last holdouts in the divisional HQ, located in an air raid shelter in the Lousberg district, surrender at 1205 hours on October 21.

THE SECOND BATTLE OF AACHEN, OCTOBER 7–21, 1944

The US First Army encircles Aachen from the east before the final street fighting.

Note: Gridlines are shown at intervals of 1.6 km (1 mile)

US UNITS

XIX Corps
1   2nd Armored Division
2   Combat Command A
3   Combat Command B
4   30th Infantry Division
5   117th Infantry
6   119th Infantry
7   120th Infantry
8   116th Infantry (attached from 29th Division)

VII Corps
9   1106th Engineer Group
10 1st Infantry Division
11 16th Infantry
12 18th Infantry
13 26th Infantry
13a 2/26th Infantry
13b 3/26th Infantry
14 3rd Armored Division
15 9th Infantry Division

Col Gerhard Wilck, commander of the 275th Infantry Division responsible for the defense of Aachen, is seen here with his staff following the surrender on October 21. (NARA)

Kampfgruppe Rink from SS-PGR 1 attempted to evacuate their wounded out of Aachen on October 20 using their surviving SdKfz 251 half-tracks, but were captured by a US tank roadblock on Oststrasse in Kohlscheid. (NARA)

Strasse started around dusk, and, after about two hours of fighting the 2/26th Infantry, the German infantry battalion was repulsed with significant casualties on both sides. As 3/26th Infantry approached the hotel, SS-Battalion Rink attacked and drove the US infantry back. After a two-day lull, the US attack resumed on October 18; they regained the lost ground, and assaulted Hotel Quellenhof. To conduct this final clearing operation, 3/26th Infantry was reinforced by Task Force Hogan from the 3rd Armored Division with an armored infantry battalion and parts of a tank battalion. Task Force Hogan attacked Lousberg from the west while 3/26th attacked through Salvatorberg from the east, both prongs meeting around noon on October 19. The last hold-outs were ensconced near the divisional HQ in an air-raid shelter in Lousberg, where they were trapped by the 2/26th Infantry. An M12 155mm GMC was driven up to the site to blast it open, but Col Wilck surrendered moments before. The surrender of the garrison officially took place at 1205 hours on October 21. About 1,600 German troops surrendered at the end, bringing the total number of German prisoners of war to 3,473 out of the original garrison of about 5,000. In addition, US troops evacuated about 6,000 civilians during the course of the fighting, and a further 1,000 after the surrender.

PRELUDE TO OPERATION *QUEEN*: HÜRTGEN

The capture of Aachen consolidated the US First and Ninth armies' positions, and set the stage for an offensive to reach the River Rhine. On October 18, 1944, Bradley and Montgomery met Eisenhower at his headquarters to discuss plans for November. In spite of shortages of supplies and infantry, Eisenhower was insistent that the Germans enjoy no

respite from Allied attack and laid out a plan for a broad-front attack in November aimed at bringing the Allied forces up to the Roer in anticipation of a subsequent push to the Rhine. For Bradley's 12th Army Group, the plan was to employ all three armies in a concerted attack with the final objective being a bridgehead over the Rhine south of Cologne. Hodges' First Army was scheduled to launch its attack, Operation *Queen*, on November 5, with the focus being in the center with Collins' VII Corps.

What would prove to be the most controversial element of the plan was in fact one of its secondary efforts – a preliminary operation to push through the towns in the center of the Hürtgen forest. The desire to clear this area of the Hürtgen forest had several tactical goals: it was the first step in clearing a pathway to the key road junction at Düren and providing the First Army with tactical maneuver room beyond the constricted Stolberg corridor; and it would serve to undermine lingering German defense of the Monschau area by threatening them from the rear. Beyond the tactical rationale, Hodges and Collins were both uncomfortable with their flanks exposed to possible German counter-attacks out of the forest, though given the terrain conditions this threat was remote. The 9th Infantry Division had already pushed through the western part of the woods, but the attack stalled after reaching the open ridgeline that controlled the road from Hürtgen, through Kleinhau and Grosshau, which provided access to the River Roer plain in front of Düren. The expectation was that this mission would take a few days, since German resistance in the sector was expected to be limited to a few battered infantry elements of the 275th Infantry Division numbering only about 3,350 troops. The Hürtgen operation was scheduled to be launched on November 2, three days before the main assault, so that once the mission was completed, another attack could be launched through the town of Hürtgen, and then northward to Düren. Since the 9th Infantry Division was spent, the corps boundaries were shifted, with Gerow's V Corps taking over the Hürtgen sector and substituting the 28th Division for the 9th Infantry Division.

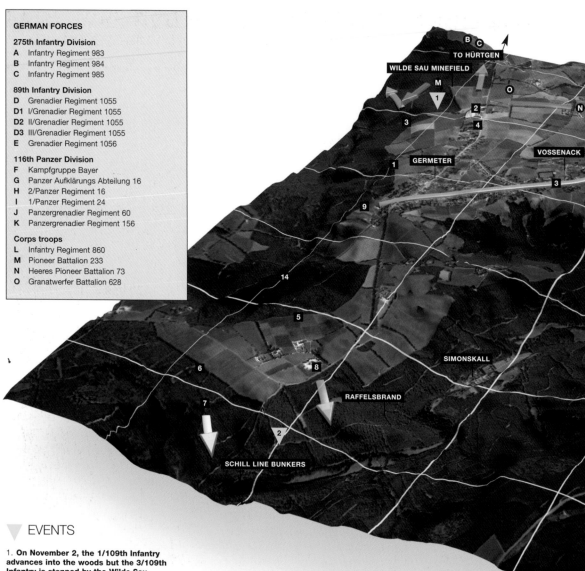

GERMAN FORCES

275th Infantry Division
A   Infantry Regiment 983
B   Infantry Regiment 984
C   Infantry Regiment 985

89th Infantry Division
D   Grenadier Regiment 1055
D1 I/Grenadier Regiment 1055
D2 II/Grenadier Regiment 1055
D3 III/Grenadier Regiment 1055
E   Grenadier Regiment 1056

116th Panzer Division
F   Kampfgruppe Bayer
G   Panzer Aufklärungs Abteilung 16
H   2/Panzer Regiment 16
I   1/Panzer Regiment 24
J   Panzergrenadier Regiment 60
K   Panzergrenadier Regiment 156

Corps troops
L   Infantry Regiment 860
M   Pioneer Battalion 233
N   Heeres Pioneer Battalion 73
O   Granatwerfer Battalion 628

▼ EVENTS

1. On November 2, the 1/109th Infantry advances into the woods but the 3/109th Infantry is stopped by the Wilde Sau minefield. The German engineers counterattack.

2. On November 2, the 110th Infantry is stopped by the Westwall bunkers of the Schill Line around Raffelsbrand.

3. On November 2, the 2/112th Infantry advances with tank support through Vossenack, placing two of its three companies in trenches in the fields east of the town and one in the town itself.

4. On November 3, the 3/112th Infantry moves through the Kall ravine to Schmidt, while the 1/112th Infantry takes up positions in Kommerscheidt.

5. The narrow trail through the Kall ravine restricts tank movement to support the 112th Infantry in Schmidt, but three M4 tanks of Company A, 707th Tank Battalion arrive on November 4, with the rest of the company trapped on the trail.

6. Attacks by PGR 156 begin on Vossenack on the morning of November 4, which is unable to break into the town. However, the exposed companies outside town take a pounding from German artillery.

7. On November 4, Schmidt is attacked from three sides by elements of the 89th Infantry Division, supported by Sturmgeschütz Brigade 341. The last defenders of 3/112th Infantry hold out in the southern part of the town until finally overrun in the early afternoon, when nine PzKpfw IV tanks of 2/Panzer Regiment 16 arrive to assist the assault.

8. In late afternoon of November 4, 2/Panzer Regiment 16 and the assault guns of StuG Brigade 341 charge out of Schmidt to assault Kommerscheidt, but take heavy losses and pull back to Schmidt.

9. On November 6, Task Force Ripple including the 3/110th Infantry attempts to reinforce Kommerscheidt, and is the last force to arrive before the Germans seal off the ravine.

10. While the US 20th Engineer Battalion continues its attempts to improve the Kall ravine trail, Panzer Aufklärungs Abteilung 16 and GR 1056 attempt to seal the Kall ravine by taking control of the Mestrenger Mill, which controls the only bridge over the river in this area. The Mestrenger Mill is finally secured by III/GR 1056 on November 6.

11. A predawn attack on Vossenack by the two Panzergrenadier regiments of the 116th Panzer Division is delayed, but the bombardment of the two outlying companies of the 2/112th Infantry leads to a disorganized rout back into town. The Panzergrenadiers move into the eastern portions of the town around noon, and house-to-house fighting continues throughout the center after dark.

12. The 146th Engineer Battalion is sent into Vossenack to reinforce the collapsing 2/112th Infantry; most of the Panzergrenadiers are forced out of the town on November 7. The town defenses are subsequently taken over by the 2/109th Infantry.

13. On November 7, Kommerscheidt is assaulted by Kampfgruppe Bayer and GR 1055, while PzAA 16 and GR 1056 advance from the rear through the Kall ravine. The US defenses in Kommerscheidt collapse after a four-hour battle.

THE HÜRTGENWALD, NOVEMBER 2–7, 1944

The battle for Schmidt and Vossenack by the 28th Infantry Division.

Note: Gridlines are shown at intervals of 1.6 km (1 mile)

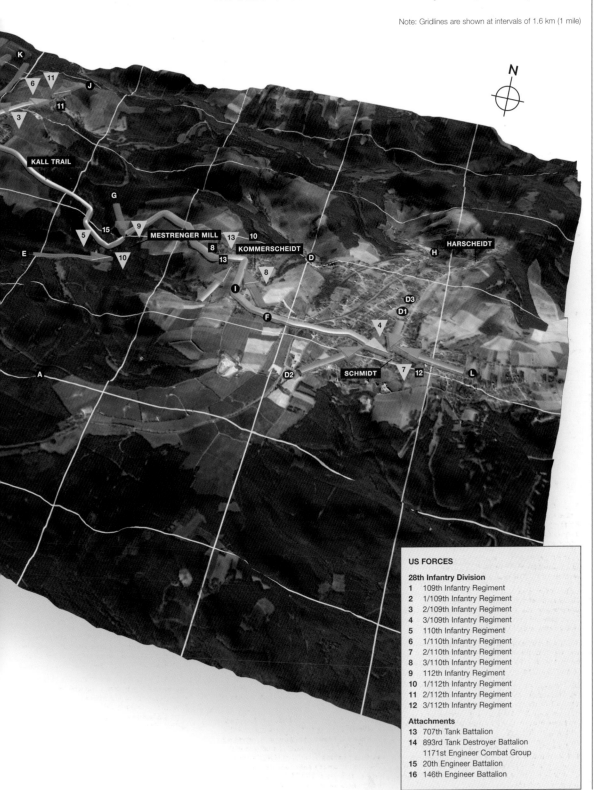

US FORCES

28th Infantry Division
1. 109th Infantry Regiment
2. 1/109th Infantry Regiment
3. 2/109th Infantry Regiment
4. 3/109th Infantry Regiment
5. 110th Infantry Regiment
6. 1/110th Infantry Regiment
7. 2/110th Infantry Regiment
8. 3/110th Infantry Regiment
9. 112th Infantry Regiment
10. 1/112th Infantry Regiment
11. 2/112th Infantry Regiment
12. 3/112th Infantry Regiment

Attachments
13. 707th Tank Battalion
14. 893rd Tank Destroyer Battalion
    1171st Engineer Combat Group
15. 20th Engineer Battalion
16. 146th Engineer Battalion

The 28th Division's three regiments covered a front about three miles wide, and each was assigned a separate mission. The northernmost regiment, the 109th Infantry, was assigned to push north towards Hürtgen as a feint and to secure a launch point for a subsequent attack on Hürtgen. The 112th Infantry in the center was assigned to launch the main attack: a two-pronged drive through Vossenack with the second thrust pushing southeast to capture Schmidt. The 110th Infantry to the south was assigned to push into the clearing east of Lammersdorf in order to secure roads to eventually reinforce and supply the 112th Infantry in Schmidt, since there were hardly any useful roads between Vossenack and Schmidt aside from a single dirt trail up the sides of the River Kall ravine. The plan underestimated the German defensive potential in the woods and the difficulties of conducting infantry operations in the mountainous forest.

In the meantime, the Germans were reconfiguring their dispositions near the Hürtgenwald (Hürtgen forest), expecting an American attack at any time. On October 22, the 5th Panzer Army was brought in to take over 7th Army's left flank from Geilenkirchen to Düren, including the western edge of the Hürtgen forest. This was necessary due to the increasing importance of the Aachen sector and the overextension of the 7th Army. This created some tactical issues, since the boundary between the two armies ran along the 81st and 74th Corps boundaries through the forest. As a result, on November 2, the staffs of both armies along with key commanders were brought together by GFM Model at Castle Schlenderhan to conduct a command-post exercise to game possible responses to a US attack near the corps boundaries in the Hürtgenwald. Coincidentally, this occurred at the same time as the US attack, and the initial German response was facilitated by the presence of so many commanders together with Model.

The German perspective of the Hürtgenwald was significantly different from the US appreciation. The senior German commanders anticipated that the principal US mission would be to strike immediately northward to seize the open ridgeline and the associated road network stretching from

An M10 3in. GMC of the 893rd Tank Destroyer Battalion moves forward along a firebreak in the Hürtgenwald west of Germeter on November 4, in an attempt to reinforce the 112th Infantry. (NARA)

Hürtgen through Kleinhau and Grosshau as an avenue to reach Düren. As a result, German defenses opposite the US 28th Division were heaviest along its northern shoulder. Two of the 275th Infantry Division's regiments were located there as well as a corps engineer battalion, working on the Wilde Sau ("Boar") minefield blocking Hürtgen. The Germans were also concerned about the presence of dams in the Hürtgenwald linked to the Schwammenauel Reservoir, which controlled the water flow into the plains around Düren along the River Roer. Should the US Army advance over the Roer without first controlling the dams, the Wehrmacht could unleash the dams and flood the Roer plain. This had not yet been appreciated by Hodges and the US First Army, though it would later play a key role in prolonging the fighting in the Hürtgen forest.

The German tactical approach to combat in the Hürtgen forest was also different from the American appreciation. Based on the September fighting between the 89th Infantry Division and the US 9th Infantry Division, the German commanders believed that it was most prudent to defend from the forest not the towns, since this denied the US Army two of its most potent weapons – air support and artillery. The autumn weather was already greatly limiting Allied air operations, but the forested defenses were very difficult to identify and strike from the air even on clear days. Artillery was not very effective in wooded areas against troops deployed in log-reinforced dugouts, since the rounds detonated in the trees overhead, and the log roofs protected the occupants from the shrapnel. In contrast, German artillery was very effective against attacking American infantry. Exposed infantrymen were very vulnerable to the overhead artillery bursts and the artillery's lethality was increased by the spray of tree splinters.

The 28th Division began its assault on November 2, but the attacks on either wing progressed poorly from the outset. The 109th Infantry was immediately halted in the Wilde Sau minefield and counterattacked through the woods by the German engineers. On the southern wing, the 110th Infantry immediately encountered the defensive bunkers of the

THE HÜRTGENWALD DEFENSES, SEPTEMBER 1944
(pages 54–55)

This scene shows a typical Hürtgenwald defense line such as that occupied by the German 89th Infantry Division while fighting against the US 9th Infantry Division in September 1944. In this case, the defense hinges on a Westwall machine-gun bunker (1). There were relatively few bunkers built in the Hürtgenwald due to the difficulties of the terrain, and they were generally positioned to cover key firebreaks, river crossing points, roads, or other significant objectives. In many cases, accompanying trenches were built at the same time as the bunkers, though in other cases they were constructed in August–September 1944 when an effort was made to refresh the Westwall after years of neglect. The trenches (2) are log-lined to prevent their collapse during the incessant autumn rains. They were dug in a zigzag fashion to limit the damage caused either by a shell impact or the intrusion of enemy infantry. In the case of a straight trench, the artillery blast would devastate the whole section of trench, or an enemy infantry attack could likewise wipe out a whole detachment if exposed in a straight line. These trenches also had small log-covered bunkers (3) either built into the trench line itself or located nearby to provide the infantry with cover from artillery attack. Although not visible here, there were usually minefields emplaced some distance in front of the trench line, and on occasion, barbed-wire entanglements were added to cover especially important defensive positions. Infantry defenses in the Hürtgenwald typically took advantage of hills, as seen here, since they provided the defenders with firepower advantages as well as presenting an attacking infantry force with greater difficulty in reaching the objective. Forest defenses were particularly effective against the US Army since they minimized the US advantage in artillery and airpower. Artillery strikes tended to detonate in the high fir trees above. While this could enhance the blast and splinter effect against exposed infantry, it actually had less effect on defenders in log bunkers than did detonations on the ground. Likewise the forest provided cover against air observation, which limited the effect of close air support. Eventually, the incessant fighting and repeated artillery strikes in the Hürtgenwald stripped away much of the tree cover, denuding the slopes and exposing the defensive trenches to artillery fire. The infantry here shows the gradual shifts in firepower evident in the autumn of 1944, with wider use of Panzerfaust antitank rockets (4) and new weapons such as the MP44 assault rifle (5).

Schill Line around Raffelsbrand, and soon became caught up in the barbed-wire entanglements under intense machine-gun fire from the German bunkers and dugouts.

The central American thrust by the 112th Infantry encountered little opposition at first. The 2/112th Infantry was able to advance with tank support along the Germeter–Vossenack road towards Schmidt. Having captured Vossenack without undue problem, the battalion took up defensive positions with one company in the town itself and the two other companies in a defensive semicircle in the fields east of the town under the enemy-controlled heights of Bergstein. This disposition would prove to be a tragic mistake as it left most of the defenders in open trenches exposed to the miserable cold and autumn rains with little protection against German artillery fire except for their water-logged trenches.

The 112th Infantry commander, Col Carl Peterson, began the advance to Schmidt the following day with his other two battalions. There was no real road between Vossenack and Schmidt, only a narrow, winding dirt track through the forested Kall ravine. On November 3, the 3/112th Infantry moved through the Kall ravine and proceeded into Schmidt, with the 1/112th following behind and occupying Kommerscheidt.

With the German staffs conferring with Model at the time, the Wehrmacht response was unusually swift. With news of the attack towards Schmidt rather than Hürtgen, Model presumed that the Americans were heading for the dams and so had to be stopped. Unhappily for the US 28th Division, the German 74th Corps was in the process of pulling out the 89th Infantry Division for refitting from the sector south of the US attack and replacing them with the 272nd VGD. Although the 89th Division was badly understrength, it was readily at hand and familiar with the local terrain, having fought around Vossenack and Schmidt a month earlier against the US 9th Infantry Division. The 89th Division was ordered to turn around and recapture Schmidt. Since the rest of the Aachen front was quiet, Model agreed to reinforce the 89th Division with the sector's best mobile reserve, the 116th Panzer Division, which was refitting east of Düren. The Panzer Aufklärungs Abteilung 116 (Armored Reconnaissance Regiment 116) was the first element of the division to arrive in the area. It was fairly well equipped by Wehrmacht standards with about 785 men, eleven SdKfz 234 heavy armored cars, 53 SdKfz 251 personnel half-tracks, and 30 SdKfz 250 light half-tracks. The rest of the division followed behind. At the time, the division was at 83 percent of authorized strength, with about 12,550 men and over 50 Panzers. The division's mechanized Panzergrenadier regiment, PGR 60, had 94 SdKfz 251 half-tracks, while its other regiment, PGR 156, was truck-borne.

The 3/112th Infantry in Schmidt was without tank support due to the poor road network in the area. Three tanks finally made their way up the Kall ravine trail to Kommerscheidt around dawn on November 4, but in the process several other tanks lost their tracks and effectively blocked the trail for any further reinforcements.

The German counterattack began on the morning of November 4. Despite the commander's complaints, a hasty attack was launched by Panzergrenadiers of the 116th Panzer Division against Vossenack, but this failed to make much progress and was forced back to its start line by determined US infantry defenses stiffened by tank support. However,

The sole link between the battalions at Kommerscheidt was this narrow dirt trail up the side of the Kall ravine, barely wide enough for a tank to pass. Several tanks became bogged down on the trail after losing their tracks, blocking it at critical moments during the battle. Their tracks can still be seen here littering the sides of the hill, weeks after the fighting has ended. (NARA)

the 2/112th Infantry took a pounding all day long from an extensive array of German artillery, including the divisional artillery of both the 275th Infantry Division and 116th Panzer Division as well as Volks Artillery Corps 766, Granatwerfer Battalion 628 with 21cm rockets, and Sturmgeschütz Brigade 394.

Schmidt was much more vulnerable to counterattack, being at a road junction. The town was hit from three sides by elements of the 89th Infantry Division supported by Sturmgeschütz Brigade 341; the US battalion in Schmidt was outnumbered by over three to one. Aside from a small number of antitank mines, the only antitank defenses in the town were bazookas, and these proved ineffective against the attacking assault guns. By noon, the German infantry had seized the northern and western portions of Schmidt, and a last-ditch defense of the south-eastern corner of the town was finally overrun in the afternoon with the arrival of nine PzKpfw IV tanks of 2/Panzer Regiment 16. With the momentum of the attack in their favor, the Panzers and assault guns charged out of Schmidt towards Kommerscheidt. The 1/112th Infantry defenses in Kommerscheidt were backed by three M4 tanks; three PzKpfw IV tanks were knocked out in quick succession and a fourth became trapped in a swamp even before reaching the town. The Panzers barreled into Kommerscheidt without infantry support and quickly lost three more in a short-range duel with the Shermans. The Panzers were forced to withdraw with their surviving five vehicles.

General Cota ordered Peterson to counterattack and retake Schmidt, a remarkably unrealistic order in the circumstances. The 1/112th

Infantry was entirely exposed in Kommerscheidt, connected to the rest of the division by the thin muddy trail up the Kall ravine. The Panzer Aufklärungs Abteilung (PzAA) 116 made numerous attempts to cut this link starting on November 4, and the trail and the nearby river bridge at the Mestrenger Mill changed hands several times during the fighting on November 5. The attack by PzAA 116 was reinforced in the other direction by the Grenadier Regiment (GR) 1056 of the 89th Division, which had been slow to arrive due to the lack of roads in the area. The combined forces of the reconnaissance battalion and GR 1056 were ordered to capture the Mestrenger Mill, which controlled the only bridge over the River Kall. After prolonged fighting with US engineer units in the ravine, the Mestrenger Mill was finally secured on November 6. In an attempt to regain Schmidt, Cota formed Task Force Ripple around the 3/110th Infantry, which moved through the ravine on November 6 and established a defensive line behind Kommerscheidt near the edge of the woods. The ravine remained a confused no-man's land, with German units intermingled with American units in the rough hills and foliage.

The 2/112th Infantry in Vossenack remained under assault for most of November 5, but the terrain made it much more difficult for the Germans to mass forces, and US artillery was able to break up some of the attempts. The attacks on Vossenack eventually involved both Panzergrenadier regiments of the 116th Panzer Division. The situation here was reaching breaking point due to the intense German artillery bombardment and the badly exposed positions of two of the three infantry companies in the rain-soaked fields outside the town. When a new company commander arrived on the scene to visit his exposed platoons, he found the troops in such a poor state that he wanted them all withdrawn for combat fatigue. The situation was not helped by the regimental headquarters, which reported back to divisional head-quarters that it was still in excellent combat condition.

The 116th Panzer Division was ordered to launch a pre-dawn attack on Vossenack around 0400 hours on November 6 using the I/PGR 60 from the southeast and II/PGR 156 from the northeast, but the regrouping in the hills under rainy conditions delayed the attack by several hours. Nevertheless, an intense 30-minute bombardment took place anyway, pounding the exposed trenches outside the town one more time. Following the barrage, rumors began to spread through the beleaguered US infantry that the Germans had broken through and in the darkness, chaos broke out. As troops fled back into the town, they set off a wave of panic that peeled back platoon after platoon. Officers managed to hold back about 70 men, but most of the two companies fled back to Germeter. After days of mind-numbing artillery bombardment in water-logged trenches, rumors and exhaustion nearly led to the loss of the town. The German attack finally began around noon, conducted by two companies from the II/PGR 156. In the meantime, the US 146th Engineer Battalion was rushed into the town as improvised infantry. The I/PGR 156 attempted to reinforce the attack from the northwest, but heavy US artillery fire pushed it back. House-to-house fighting continued until well after dusk, with the Panzergrenadiers finally capturing the town church shortly before midnight. On November 7, the 146th Engineer Battalion counterattacked the remaining Panzergrenadiers of the 116th Panzer Division, who had fought their way into the eastern side of Vossenack

Eisenhower visits Gen Norman Cota's headquarters to conduct a postmortem on what had gone so terribly wrong in the Hürtgen fighting. Cota (right) wears the keystone insignia of the 28th Division based on its origins with the Pennsylvania National Guard. After Hürtgen, the insignia was grimly known as the "bloody bucket." (NARA)

around the church. By the end of the day, most of the town had been retaken with heavy German losses. Nevertheless, US losses had been far more severe. The extent of them within the 2/112th Infantry is evident from the pace of replacements: the battalion received 515 reinforcements on November 8 alone. The heavy losses suffered by the 28th Division had forced the V Corps to take notice and on November 7, the 4th Infantry Division dispatched its 12th Infantry to take over the 109th Infantry positions in anticipation of further attacks against Hürtgen but from positions further north. This permitted the dispatch of 2/109th Infantry to Vossenack to take over the positions abandoned by the 2/112th Infantry.

On November 6, the 89th Infantry Division began organizing for a renewed counterattack against Kommerscheidt with Panzer support, while PzAA 116 along with GR 1056 cut off the US positions from behind through the Kall ravine. The attack began around dawn on November 7 from two directions. The fighting lasted for four hours, finally pushing the last US troops out of the town. In the meantime, the 28th Division had tried to form another task force under the assistant divisional commander, Brig Gen George Davis, but the force reached the Kall ravine only after Kommerscheidt had already fallen. Later that day, the remaining defenses east of the Kall were pulled back after Cota received permission from First Army. The disaster that had befallen the 28th Division led to a visit by all the senior US Army brass, including Eisenhower, Bradley, Hodges and Gerow. Divisional casualties to date had been 6,184, with the hapless 112th Infantry having suffered 2,093 battle casualties, as well as 544 non-battle casualties from combat exhaustion and trench foot. Total German casualties in this phase of the Hürtgenwald fighting were 2,900, and the 116th Panzer Division alone needed 1,800 replacements with GR 1055 needing 490.

The reasons for the debacle were many. To begin with, the attack plan dispersed the 28th Division on three separate and unco-ordinated missions leaving each regiment isolated. With two of the regiments tied down in the German defenses on the shoulders, this left the 112th Infantry exposed to the full force of two German divisions. The isolation of the battalions of the 112th Infantry due to the terrain allowed the Germans to destroy the 112th Infantry piecemeal, a battalion at a time. The dispositions of the 2/112th Infantry in Vossenack were poor, and Kommerscheidt's isolation due to the Kall trail made it unusually vulnerable. The decision to postpone Operation *Queen* from November 5 to November 16 due to the poor weather doomed the 28th Division, since it allowed the German 7th Army to throw all of its reserves into the Hürtgenwald. This included a considerable amount of artillery, which was instrumental in reducing the 112th Infantry positions in Kommerscheidt and Vossenack, and also permitted the participation of the 7th Army's operational reserve, the 116th Panzer Division.

OPERATION *QUEEN*

Bradley's major autumn offensive, Operation *Queen*, was scheduled to begin on November 5, but was repeatedly delayed until November 16. The principal problem was the rainy and overcast weather that prevented the planned air strike, larger than any previous Allied air effort in the ETO. Bradley saw Operation *Queen* as a replay of Operation *Cobra* in Normandy, a massive air strike paving the way for a quick US Army breakthrough out of congested terrain into open tank country for a deep envelopment of German defenses. As in the case of *Cobra*, the starring role was given to the First Army and especially Collins' VII Corps, which would push out of the Stolberg corridor towards the Roer. In the meantime, Gerow's V Corps would be given the unenviable task of

The Roer front in November was a sea of mud, leading to many improvisations. Here, GIs of the 9th Division help the crew of an M4 tank of the 746th Tank Battalion attach a section of corduroy matting on the front of the tank on December 10 prior to the attack on Merode. The matting consisted of several logs tied together with wire and could be laid down as a carpet in front of the tank when particularly deep mud was encountered. (NARA)

OPERATION *QUEEN*: NOVEMBER 16–DECEMBER 9, 1944

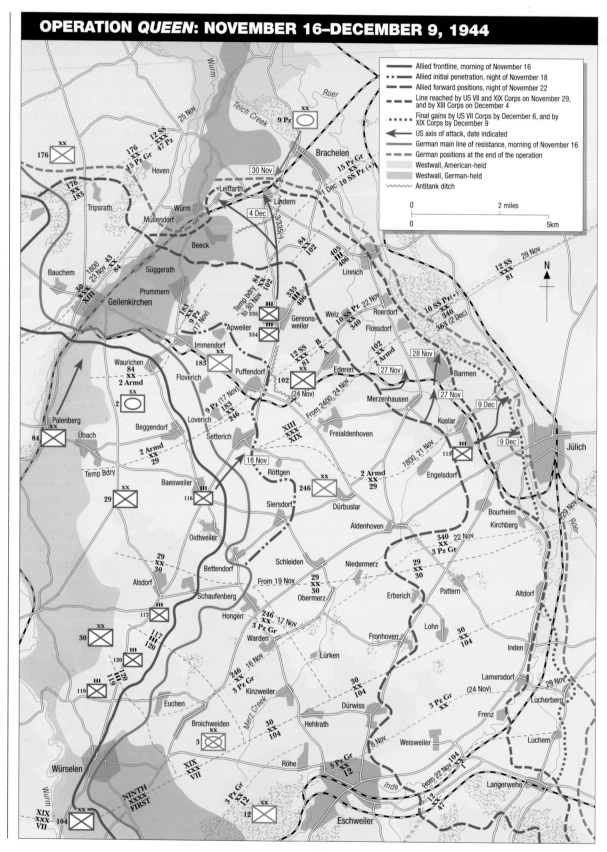

Legend:
- Allied frontline, morning of November 16
- Allied initial penetration, night of November 18
- Allied forward positions, night of November 22
- Line reached by US VII and XIX Corps on November 29, and by XIII Corps on December 4
- Final gains by US VII Corps by December 6, and by XIX Corps by December 9
- US axis of attack, date indicated
- German main line of resistance, morning of November 16
- German positions at the end of the operation
- Westwall, American-held
- Westwall, German-held
- Antitank ditch

0 — 2 miles
0 — 5km

continuing to push back the German defenses along the edge of the Hürtgen forest towards Düren. The battleground for the First Army advance was constricted by the terrain, hilly and heavily urbanized in the VII Corps sector, and the forested hell of the Hürtgen in the V Corps sector. This time, two infantry divisions would be committed to the Hürtgen, the 1st to clear the northeastern fringes, and the 4th to attack straight into the forest to seize Hürtgen and the roads to Düren. By this stage the US Army had finally begun to appreciate the importance of the Roer dams in the forest, and Operation *Queen* presumed that the offensive would have to be halted along the Roer until the problem of the dams was settled.

Simpson's neighboring Ninth Army was given the mission of pushing its forces up to the Roer on the left flank. The terrain in the Ninth Army sector was in some respects more favorable for advance, consisting of relatively flat farmland interrupted by many villages. The greatest challenge was the town of Geilenkirchen, positioned in the midst of a dense concentration of Westwall bunkers and sitting on the border between the US 12th Army Group and the British–Canadian 21st Army Group.

The German defenses in the sector had gradually improved, but were still operating on a minimum of forces while the best units were pulled back for refitting prior to the Ardennes offensive. Manteuffel's 5th Panzer Army had taken over the northwestern sector for three weeks in late October, but, since it was an essential element of the Ardennes plans, the headquarters was pulled out and replaced by Zangen's 15th Army under the phoney name of "Gruppe von Manteuffel" on the eve of the US offensive. During the lull in fighting in late October, the emphasis in this sector was to improve the defenses with mines, entrenched antitank guns, and redoubts for the infantry to protect them against artillery. Model's operational objective was to keep the US Army bottled up west of the Roer. If the situation with the German infantry and Panzer units in the area was not particularly good, German artillery in the sector was relatively ample; a one-time issue of artillery ammunition from the Führer reserve was allotted to the 81st Corps, though this would be exhausted in a few days of heavy fighting. Like most of the industrialized areas of Germany, there were numerous heavy flak batteries, which made potent antitank weapons.

Operation *Queen*: VII Corps

Collins' VII Corps faced three German divisions in the Stolberg corridor: the 3rd Panzergrenadier Division, 12th VGD and 246th VGD. Two of these divisions had been fighting in this sector since September; the 12th VGD having been renamed by Hitler to honor its earlier performance. The 246th VGD had been resurrected after the surrender of its previous namesake in Aachen the month before. The 12th VGD was scheduled for replacement by the 47th VGD for refitting, and suffered the misfortune of carrying this out in the midst of the US attack. The 47th VGD had been rebuilt recently with half its infantry coming from the Luftwaffe and navy, and the other half from fresh 17–18-year-old recruits with only six weeks' training.

The preliminary air bombardment on November 16 was directed mainly against the towns along the Roer. Heavy bombers from the US Eight Air Force delivered 4,120 tons and the RAF a further 5,640 tons. Air strikes by medium bombers and fighter-bombers were much more limited due to the lingering overcast. The air attacks did not have the dramatic effects of the Operation *Cobra* attacks since they were not directed against the German frontline positions. While the attacks certainly laid waste to several German towns, they caused very modest casualties among the Wehrmacht infantry. The main tactical effect was to severely disrupt German tactical communications, which relied heavily on wire and telephone networks that were shredded by the attack.

The only unit badly hit by the attack was the hapless 47th VGD, which happened to be coming off trains in stations along the line just as the bombers hit. One of its artillery battalions was annihilated in Jülich, the headquarters and support battalions were smashed up in Düren, and a number of infantry battalions were in the bomb zone as well. A seasoned German NCO later recalled the effect on the recent recruits: "I never saw anything like it. These kids were still numb 45 minutes after the bombardment. It was lucky that [the Americans] didn't attack us until the next day. I could have done nothing with my boys that day." The air attack was followed by a massive artillery preparation with the First Army firing some 45,000 light, 4,000 medium and 2,600 heavy rounds.

The VII Corps attack was conducted by the 1st Infantry Division on the right and the 104th Division on the left. The 104th Division was a recent arrival in the theater, commanded by "Terrible Terry" Allen who had commanded the 1st Division in North Africa and Sicily before running afoul of senior commanders for his pugnacious personality. The 1st Division attack made slow but steady progress against the fresh but inexperienced 47th VGD around the village of Hamich on the edge of the Hürtgen forest. A counterattack with support from the 116th Panzer Division was conducted on the night of November 18, but in the dark two battalions of GR 104 of the 47th VGD stumbled into US positions near Hamich and were decimated by small-arms fire and artillery. Nevertheless, the wretched autumn weather and appalling forest conditions assisted the 47th VGD's defense, and, after four days of fighting, the 1st Division had penetrated only about two miles into the forest at a cost of a thousand casualties.

Collins planned to use CCA, 3rd Armored Division to support the 104th Division while CCB would operate independently to take a series of villages along the northwestern fringe of the Hürtgen, defended by their old adversary, the 12th VGD. The CCB tank advance was hampered by the mud and by the skillful deployment of long-range flak guns on the heights around Eschweiler. The hilly terrain on the route of advance gave the German defenders excellent observation of the approach routes of CCB, and a heavy toll was taken on half-track infantry and tanks alike. Although the CCB secured its initial objectives in three days, the casualties were appalling – about half the men in the two companies of armored infantry, and 49 of the 69 tanks. The causes of the tank losses give some sense of the nature of the fighting: six were lost to Panzerfausts, 12 to mines, 24 to guns, and six to field artillery.

Pvt Robert Starkey of the 16th Infantry, 1st Infantry Division stands beside the burnt-out hulk of a Pzkpfw IV/70. Starkey knocked out this tank with his bazooka during the fighting near Hamich, Germany on November 22.

A rifleman of the 104th Division prepares to fire a rifle grenade from his M1 Garand rifle during the fighting for Stolberg on November 16, 1944.

The 1st Infantry Division committed its reserves to a renewed attack past the industrialized Langerwehe–Jüngersdorf corridor. The 18th and the 26th Infantry remained engulfed in the fighting in the northwestern tip of the Hürtgen forest with predictably slow progress and painful casualties. The 18th Infantry battered its way past Heistern and approached Langerwehe through the woods. The 16th Infantry and the attached 47th Infantry fought to the west, in an area where the Hürtgen forest gradually gives way to the more open terrain of the Roer plain. Once again, the landscape was dominated by hills that overlooked the approach routes of the 1st Division and made it possible for the Germans to use their artillery effectively to stymie the advance. The defenders on Hill 187 near Nothberg proved to be particularly nettlesome opponents, and in sheer frustration the VII Corps authorized the use of virtually all the corps artillery – some 20 battalions, including a 240mm howitzer battalion – to blast the 300-yard crest for three minutes on November 21. When a US patrol made its way up the slope 12 hours later, they found nothing but the dead and 80 German soldiers too dazed to resist.

Collins began to realize that his hope for a quick breakthrough to the Roer had evaporated, so he began to use his exploitation reserve, the 3rd Armored Division, to facilitate the breakthrough. Task Force Richardson from CCA, 3rd Armored Division was added to the 47th Infantry and positioned in the open ground near Nothberg for an advance along the 1st Division's left flank. In spite of the armored support, the attack was slow due to the mud, extensive minefields, and well-positioned German antitank guns. Following the capture of the castle at Frenzerburg, the Germans staged a vigorous counterattack. What alarmed the 1st Division was that these troops were from the 3rd Fallschirmjäger Division, the first major injection of German reinforcements into this sector since the beginning of Operation *Queen*. Rundstedt had only consented to its transfer from Holland if two other divisions could be pulled back for refitting for the Ardennes attack. In this case, the 12th and 47th VGD had been bled white in the fighting over the previous two weeks, and so were finally pulled out. In spite of its name, the parachute division consisted mainly of inexperienced troops, and the substitution of this raw division created temporary opportunities for the 1st Infantry Division. After pushing past Hill 203, the 16th and 18th Infantry finally exited the forest and fought their way into the ruins of Langerwehe, subduing Jüngersdorf as well by nightfall on November 28. It proved to be far more difficult for the 26th Infantry when it tried to push out of the woods at Merode, where two companies were surrounded and wiped out on November 29 by a combined attack of the German paratroopers and Panzers. By the beginning of December, the 1st Division was a spent force, having suffered 3,993 battle casualties, and more than 2,000 non-battle casualties.

At the outset of Operation *Queen*, the 104th Division advanced into the River Inde valley aiming for the hill town of Donnerberg, which had resisted numerous previous attacks. The initial attacks against the 12th

An M4A3E2 assault tank of the 745th Tank Battalion wades through the water and mud under a destroyed railroad viaduct in early December during the fighting for the industrial town of Langerwehe by the 1st Infantry Division. (NARA)

VGD positions made little progress for the first two days of fighting, but, finally, three major bunkers were cleared on November 18, with the 414th Infantry gaining the heights. The other two regiments were kept idle until the heights were captured, and so did not begin major actions until November 19. The 413th Infantry aimed for the industrial town of Eschweiler, while the 415th Infantry was to clear the northern half of Stolberg. The 12th VGD put up a determined defense of Eschweiler, so Gen Allen decided to force them out by encircling the town. This worked, and late on November 21 Rundstedt authorized the 12th VGD to pull out of Eschweiler to more defensible positions, leaving the town open to the 104th Division. Gen Allen had taken great pains to train the division in night operations, and this came in handy on several occasions. In the renewed fighting after November 23, night attacks proved successful in cases where day attacks had faltered, as they prevented the German assault guns and direct fire artillery from observing the attack. The towns along the River Inde fell in succession, but the advance was costly due to German artillery, which at one point was firing at a rate of 50 rounds per minute. The pressure against the depleted 3rd PGD was so severe that the 246th VGD replaced the 3rd PGD in the fighting for Inden. After five days of fighting, the town was finally taken, setting the stage for crossing the River Inde towards the Roer. The main obstruction to the crossing was the town of Lucherberg, which was not secured until December 4. The next day the 3rd Fallschirmjäger Division executed a pre-dawn counterattack, but small-arms fire and an intense artillery response crushed the attack. In the three-day fight for Lucherberg, the 3rd Fallschirmjäger Division suffered about 850 casualties, compared to about 100 casualties in the 415th Infantry. The discrepancy was in no small measure due to the volume of artillery available to the 104th Division.

Operation *Queen*: the Hürtgen forest

By mid November, Bradley and the rest of the senior leadership were finally aware of the threat posed by the Roer dams, and were determined to gain control of them as well as obtain another route to Düren. The difficulties of forest fighting had still not been fully realized by the senior leadership in spite of the horrible costs inflicted on the 9th and 28th Divisions in previous fighting. There was the hope that German defenses in the forest would be weakened by the demands elsewhere on the Roer front.

The main onus fell on the 4th Infantry Division, positioned further north than the hapless 28th Division. The 4th Infantry Division's commander, Gen Raymond "Tubby" Barton, deployed the 8th Infantry on the left to cover the flank with the neighboring 1st Infantry Division from VII Corps; the 22nd Infantry was given the central task of pushing out of the forest to Grosshau on the Hürtgen ridgeline; and the 12th Infantry would maintain the right flank opposite Hürtgen in the sector formerly held by the northernmost of the 28th Division units. The intelligence assessment suggested that German forces facing them were very weak – a necessary prerequisite, since the 22nd Infantry was allotted a grossly overextended attack frontage three miles wide. In fact, this sector was defended by the 275th Infantry Division with about 6,500 troops, 106 artillery pieces, 23 antitank guns, and 21 assault guns.

The initial attempt by the 8th Infantry to advance through the woods on November 16 was an ominous repeat of the situation facing the 109th Infantry a month before. The Germans had mined the forward defense line and built up another set of wire entanglements. After failing to penetrate it the first day, a second attempt on November 17 resulted in 200 casualties in one battalion alone. As other units had learned from previous forest fighting, tank support, no matter how

GIs of the 3/8th Infantry, 4th Infantry Division move up the slopes of the Hürtgenwald along the River Wehe between Schevenhütte and Josawerk on November 18. (NARA)

A pair of M10 3in. GMC of the 803rd Tank Destroyer Battalion move up a forest trail near Josawerk in mid November while supporting the 4th Infantry Division in the fighting in the Hürtgenwald. (NARA)

Gen "Tubby" Barton, the 4th Division commander, seen here driving his jeep, confers with the commander of the 22nd Infantry, Col Charles Lanham, in mid September before the Hürtgen fighting. (NARA)

difficult to implement, was critical. On November 18, the 8th Infantry was supported by two platoons of light and medium tanks, which finally managed to blast away the obstructions. With armored support, the 8th Infantry was able to reach one of the few roads in the area.

The 22nd Infantry's zone of advance was far from ideal since there were no roads in the sector and the only hope of keeping the unit supplied would be to improve one of the firebreaks running through the forest – hardly an ideal situation in hilly, forested terrain already inundated with autumn rain. The regiment had to move through the ravine of the Weisser Weh then surmount the Rabenheck ridge. The regiment struggled for three days through the rugged terrain while encountering only an occasional German outpost. Casualties came from the numerous mines, which were especially thick along the firebreak trails, and from German artillery which already had most of the key firebreaks and crossing points zeroed in. In the first three days of the advance, the 22nd Infantry lost all three battalion commanders, half its company commanders and many other combat leaders.

In spite of the difficulties facing both regiments, by November 19 the advance appeared to be progressing steadily if slowly, and German resistance was weak. The German 7th Army reacted on the night of November 18/19, dispatching GR 1058 of the 344th VGD, and reinforcing the 275th Infantry Division positions around Grosshau. These new troops slowed the advance of the US 8th and 22nd Infantry regiments to a crawl on November 20. In the first five days of combat, both regiments had penetrated the forest to a depth of about a mile and a half but had suffered 1,500 casualties, with losses in combat leaders being especially grievous. Recognizing that the division could advance little further unless reinforced, the First Army ordered the V Corps to take over the entire Hürtgen sector and to commit another division, the 8th Infantry Division, from the positions being held by the 12th Infantry with the aim of taking the town of Hürtgen. In the meantime, the German 7th Army completed the relief of the battered 275th Infantry Division with the 344th VGD.

The commitment of the 8th Infantry Division complicated the 7th Army's defense of the Hürtgen plateau, but the advance of the 4th Infantry Division remained slow. The 8th and 22nd Infantry finally reached the woods' edge near Grosshau after employing deception. On November 22, two battalions pretended to stage an attack with gunfire, smoke and artillery support while safely ensconced in their log bunkers. This attracted the German artillery in abundance while three other battalions executed the actual attack. In spite of this small success, the

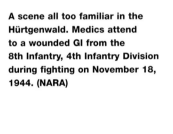

A scene all too familiar in the Hürtgenwald. Medics attend to a wounded GI from the 8th Infantry, 4th Infantry Division during fighting on November 18, 1944. (NARA)

OPERATION *QUEEN*, NOVEMBER 16–DECEMBER 9, 1944

US V Corps seizes Hürtgen and Grosshau in the Hürtgenwald.

Note: Gridlines are shown at intervals of 1.6km (1 mile)

▼ EVENTS

1. After two days of fighting with IR 1057, 8th Infantry with tank support reaches "Road V," the only road in this sector.

2. The 22nd Infantry fights its way over the Weisser Weh creek, and over the Rabenheck ridge.

3. With 275th Infantry Division too weak to resist, IR 1058 of the 344th Infantry Division is sent in to counterattack the American advance.

4. Through a ruse, 22nd Infantry fights its way to the woods' edge near Grosshau on November 22. The first attempt to take the town on November 25 fails.

5. Initial attacks by the 121st Infantry on November 21 are stopped by the Wilde Sau minefield; the attempted reinforcement by TF Boyer, CCR, 5th Armored Division on November 25 is halted by a heavily mined road.

6. The 121st Infantry fights its way to the edge of the woods around Hürtgen on November 27, and on November 28 the town is assaulted by infantry riding on the back of tanks of the 709th Tank Battalion; the town is finally captured.

7. A second assault on Grosshau on November 29 by the 22nd Infantry seems to fail after tank support is knocked out, but at nightfall tanks fight their way into town.

8. Task Force Hamberg, CCR, 5th Armored Division takes Kleinhau on November 29, opening the road to the Brandenberg plateau.

9. A major counterattack by 353rd VGD in the Gey area begins on December 2, but is beaten back by artillery.

10. The 83rd Division begins arriving on December 3 to take over the 4th Infantry Division sector.

11. After being stopped on December 2, Task Force Hamberg advances on Brandenberg and takes the town on December 3.

12. Task Force Hamberg takes Bergstein on December 5, but is counterattacked the following day by GR 980 of the 272nd VGD.

13. The 2nd Ranger Battalion attacks Castle Hill outside Bergstein held by II./GR 980 on December 7, precipitating a fierce fight for the crest against the 272nd VGD.

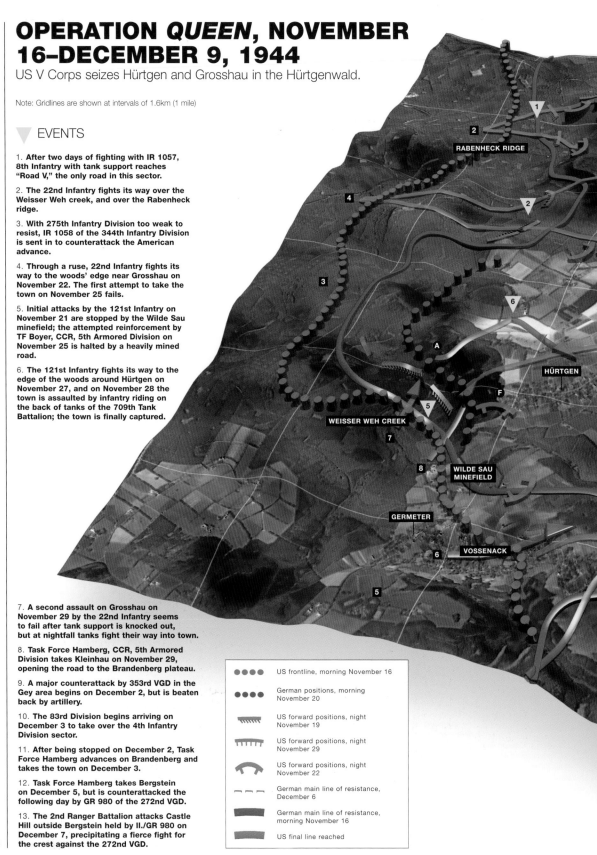

RABENHECK RIDGE

HÜRTGEN

WEISSER WEH CREEK

WILDE SAU MINEFIELD

GERMETER

VOSSENACK

●●●●	US frontline, morning November 16
●●●●	German positions, morning November 20
⌄⌄⌄⌄⌄	US forward positions, night November 19
⊓⊓⊓⊓⊓	US forward positions, night November 29
⌒	US forward positions, night November 22
− − −	German main line of resistance, December 6
▬▬▬	German main line of resistance, morning November 16
▬▬▬	US final line reached

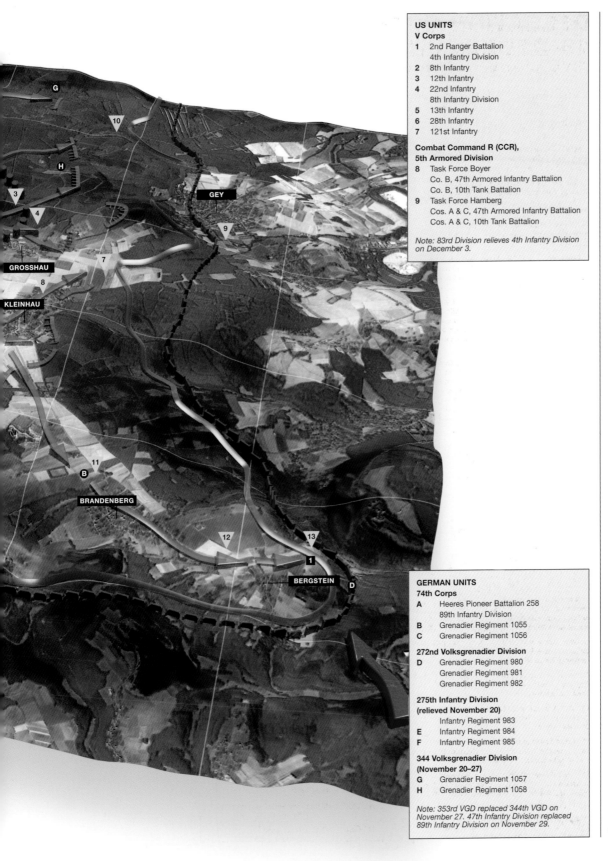

GROSSHAU

KLEINHAU

GEY

BRANDENBERG

BERGSTEIN

US UNITS
V Corps
1. 2nd Ranger Battalion
   4th Infantry Division
2. 8th Infantry
3. 12th Infantry
4. 22nd Infantry
   8th Infantry Division
5. 13th Infantry
6. 28th Infantry
7. 121st Infantry

Combat Command R (CCR),
5th Armored Division
8. Task Force Boyer
   Co. B, 47th Armored Infantry Battalion
   Co. B, 10th Tank Battalion
9. Task Force Hamberg
   Cos. A & C, 47th Armored Infantry Battalion
   Cos. A & C, 10th Tank Battalion

Note: 83rd Division relieves 4th Infantry Division on December 3.

GERMAN UNITS
74th Corps
A. Heeres Pioneer Battalion 258
   89th Infantry Division
B. Grenadier Regiment 1055
C. Grenadier Regiment 1056

272nd Volksgrenadier Division
D. Grenadier Regiment 980
   Grenadier Regiment 981
   Grenadier Regiment 982

275th Infantry Division
(relieved November 20)
   Infantry Regiment 983
E. Infantry Regiment 984
F. Infantry Regiment 985

344 Volksgrenadier Division
(November 20–27)
G. Grenadier Regiment 1057
H. Grenadier Regiment 1058

Note: 353rd VGD replaced 344th VGD on November 27. 47th Infantry Division replaced 89th Infantry Division on November 29.

This 75mm PaK 40 antitank gun was positioned to cover the road outside Kleinhau, and was captured by the 8th Division in the late November 1944 fighting. (NARA)

Battery A, 18th Field Artillery Battalion fires a salvo of 4.5in. rockets during the fighting in the Hürtgenwald on November 26. This was the only rocket artillery battalion in the US Army at the time. (NARA)

first attempt by the 22nd Infantry to seize the town of Grosshau on November 25 failed due to the usual problems of co-ordinating infantry and armor support in the wretched forest conditions. The division ordered another lull to bring up elements of the 12th Infantry and to narrow the attack sectors of the two lead regiments. During the month, the 4th Infantry Division had needed 4,924 replacements – more than double the number of riflemen in the two attacking regiments. In the two weeks of fighting, some companies had gone through three or four company commanders; platoons were now commanded by sergeants and squads by privates. In spite of the appalling level of losses, the division continued to fight on. A renewed attack on Grosshau was forced on the division, ready or not, when the neighboring 8th Division to the

Infantry of the 8th Division was finally able to break into the town of Hürtgen on November 28 riding on the back of M4 tanks of the attached 709th Tank Battalion, seen here in the ruins of Kirchstrasse. (NARA)

An 81mm mortar team from the 2/22nd Infantry, 4th Infantry Division fires in support of its battalion fighting in the woods near Grosshau, Germany on December 1. (NARA)

south was attacking Kleinhau. The initial attack on November 29 faced the usual problems with tank support. The two tanks that did emerge out of the woods were knocked out by assault guns, two more were lost to mines, and the rest got stuck in the forest bogs or blocked by uncleared minefields. Shortly before dark, the situation abruptly changed as a flanking maneuver placed troops to the northeast of the town just as a group of tanks from the 70th Tank Battalion finally made their way out of the woods. Illuminated by the burning buildings, the town was cleared in house-to-house fighting.

An M4 tank of CCR, 5th Armored Division takes up position on the northeast edge of Hürtgen prior to the renewal of the attack towards the Brandenberg–Bergstein plateau in early December 1944. (NARA)

The capture of Grosshau fundamentally altered the momentum of the attack since now the 4th Infantry Division could call on the support of CCA, 5th Armored Division to assist in the drive north along the open portions of the plateau. The timing was opportune as on December 2, the Germans launched a major counterattack from Gey, which was beaten back at the last minute by heavy artillery concentrations. By this stage of the fighting, the 4th Infantry Division commander, Gen Barton, turned to the VII Corps commander and frankly acknowledged that his division was in no shape to continue the offensive. In two weeks of combat, the division had suffered 4,053 battle casualties and over 2,000 non-battle casualties – more than twice the division's allotted strength in riflemen. Collins ordered the division to stand down, and the 83rd Division began arriving on December 3 to finish the fighting in the forest. The 4th Infantry Division was transferred to a quiet sector of the front for rebuilding – the Ardennes – where it lay directly in the path of the upcoming German offensive.

While the 4th Infantry Division was conducting its final fight for Grosshau, the newly arrived 8th Infantry Division deployed two of its regiments in the Vossenack area. The burden of the task fell on the 121st Infantry, which was allotted the mission of pushing up the road to Hürtgen. The only difference this time compared with the previous debacles of the 109th and 12th Infantry was that the 121st Infantry was allotted a combat command from the 5th Armored Division to reinforce the attack once it penetrated the initial forward German defense lines. As should have been predicted, the attack by the 121st Infantry on November 21 was immediately stopped in the Wilde Sau minefield, which had been continually refreshed by German engineers. At the time, the 7th Army was able to concentrate about eight artillery battalions against the 121st Infantry, firing on average some 3,500 rounds a day. The regimental commander tried to prod the battalions along, relieving three company commanders in a few days. But after three bloody days, the 121st Infantry had failed to reach its objectives. An attempt by tanks of CCR, 5th Armored Division on the morning of

A German Maultier half-track being used as an ambulance was abandoned along the road from Kleinhau to Brandenberg during the advance of the 121st Infantry, 8th Division in early December. (NARA)

November 25 was quickly halted by mines and antitank guns, and CCR withdrew until the road was cleared.

The 8th Division attack was renewed on November 26 after the 121st Infantry was reinforced by the 1/13th Infantry. While the US infantry had taken heavy casualties, US artillery had inflicted substantial losses on the German infantry as well. Within a day, the 121st Infantry had advanced to the woods on the western and southern side of Hürtgen. US infantry began attacking into the town of Hürtgen on November 27 while the German Fortress Machine-gun Battalion 31 continued to defend from the rubble. Finally on November 28, a company of infantry rushed the town, riding M4 tanks of the 709th Tank Battalion. House-to-house fighting ensued, but by the end of the day the town was finally in the hands of the 121st Infantry and 200 prisoners were rounded up.

With the road through Hürtgen finally clear, CCR, 5th Armored Division was ordered to try its hand against Kleinhau, the next town on the plateau, to coincide with the 4th Infantry Division attack on Grosshau. The weather permitted air strikes to supplement artillery bombardment of the town and the pilots reported that Kleinhau had been "practically destroyed by flames." Although the shoulders of the road were mined, the Germans had not had time to mine the road itself, and Task Force Hamberg pushed into the town. German artillery was much less active than usual, as the clear weather allowed US fighter-bombers to operate and attack any active batteries. By the end of the day, the 10th Tank Battalion had established roadblocks on the other side of Kleinhau facing Grosshau. The cost to the 121st Infantry and attached units in nine days of fighting had been 1,247 casualties, but the Germans had lost 882 prisoners alone and had suffered substantial additional casualties.

The importance of the capture of Kleinhau was that it opened up a route towards the Roer dams across the top of the plateau instead of through the woods beyond Vossenack. Rather than push north towards Düren, V Corps was ordered to proceed eastward to seize the

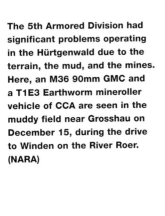

The 5th Armored Division had significant problems operating in the Hürtgenwald due to the terrain, the mud, and the mines. Here, an M36 90mm GMC and a T1E3 Earthworm mineroller vehicle of CCA are seen in the muddy field near Grosshau on December 15, during the drive to Winden on the River Roer. (NARA)

Brandenberg–Bergstein ridge, which provided a good road network that cut across the northern neck of the Hürtgen forest. Task Force Hamberg set off down the road at dawn on December 2, but was quickly stopped by a minefield covered by German guns from the Kommerscheidt–Schmidt ridge above. The weather the next day intervened in favor of the Americans and so fighter-bombers were able to keep the German artillery suppressed; Brandenberg was captured before noon. Curiously enough, after the American P-47s left, the Luftwaffe made a rare appearance and about 60 Bf-109 fighters tried to strafe the town, but with little effect.

After Bergstein fell on December 5, the 7th Army shifted two regiments of the 272nd VGD to counterattack. About 250 infantry of GR 980 supported by five Panzers attacked Bergstein before dawn on December 6, and a vicious close-range battle ensued, with the German infantry hunting down US tanks with Panzerfaust antitank rockets. As daylight arrived, the US tanks made quick work of the supporting German Panzers and the German infantry withdrew. In spite of their losses, GR 980 tried two more counterattacks later in the day, which were bloodily repulsed. V Corps dispatched one of its last reserves, the 2nd Ranger Battalion, to assist in the final push. The Rangers were assigned to capture "Castle Hill," a prominent rise beyond Bergstein where German artillery observers were directing fire against the town. A surprise attack by two companies quickly captured the crest of the hill but the Rangers were subjected to punishing artillery fire and numerous counterattacks. By noon, the two Ranger companies had been reduced to barely 32 men. Fortunately for the Rangers, they had an artillery forward observer in their midst who was able to turn the tide with accurate artillery fire. The capture of the Brandenberg-Bergstein ridge had cost the 8th Infantry Division and its attachments some 4,000 casualties, including 1,200 non-battle casualties, and the Rangers lost a quarter of their men in two days of fighting.

By the beginning of December, the First Army had fought its way through the Hürtgen forest, but at a horrible cost. Combat casualties in the four divisions most heavily involved totaled 23,000 dead, wounded, captured, and missing, plus an additional 8,000 men incapacitated by trench foot, combat fatigue, and disease. Gen Maj G. von Gersdorf, chief of staff of the 7th Army and a veteran of the Russian front, called the Hürtgen fighting the heaviest of the entire war.

Operation *Queen*: XIX Corps

During the reorganization of the front after the Aachen fighting in October, the XIX Corps became the principal element of the newly arrived US Ninth Army. The terrain in this sector was fundamentally different than in the First Army sector, consisting of relatively flat farmland interspersed with small farm villages. Indeed, GFM Model had expected the main US effort to be in this sector precisely because of the better terrain. However, Bradley decided to entrust the main thrust to VII Corps due to its greater experience, in spite of the congestion and terrain difficulties in the Stolberg corridor. The XIX Corps commander decided that to take best advantage of the terrain opportunities, the focus of the corps attack would be in the center and away from the strongest German defenses around Geilenkirchen on the left flank and

A patrol of armored infantry of the 2nd Armored Division passes a burned-out Panther of the 9th Panzer Division in Immendorf on November 16 at the start of Operation *Queen*. (NARA)

Würselen on the right flank. The corps had three experienced divisions – the 2nd Armored, and 29th and 30th Infantry divisions – and could expect the support of the 84th Division of the neighboring XIII Corps to deal with the problem of Geilenkirchen.

As in the First Army sector, Operation *Queen* began with a massive air strike that mainly hit the towns along the Roer. The 30th Division began its assault with all three regiments in line, with the expectations that the northernmost regiment, the 117th, would advance the quickest while the southernmost, the 119th Infantry, would move the slowest due to the need to clear the remainder of Würselen and its associated Westwall bunkers. The intention was to swing the division around Würselen. The opposition was the 3rd PGD, with a strength of 11,000 troops. Mines hampered the initial attacks, and, as was expected, the advance through Würselen was painfully slow compared to the other two regimental objectives. The 3rd PGD defense was undermined by the corps decision to shift boundaries northward to deal with the threat of the US VII Corps attack. It took the 30th Division four days to clear the Würselen area, suffering 535 casualties – and capturing 1,600 prisoners – in the process. As the division shifted its orientation towards the Roer, German defenses stiffened. After capturing the town of Bourheim on November 23, the advance ground to a halt. Both sides engaged in several days of attack, counterattack and heavy artillery action. The US XIX Corps averaged about 27,000 rounds a day in the last week of November, while the German 81st Corps averaged 13,400 rounds a day, which was extremely heavy by German standards. The attacks resumed on November 26 with the 30th Division being ordered to take Altdorf. The division wanted to stage a night attack due to the prevalence of German machine-gun nests and the absence of tank support due to the mud, but the corps headquarters ordered a daylight attack coinciding with the neighboring 29th Division push for Kirchberg. As predicted, the heavy German machine-gun fire halted the daylight attack, but a night attack the next evening succeeded in capturing the

OPERATION *QUEEN*: THE TANK BATTLE AT PUFFENDORF, NOVEMBER 17, 1944 (pages 78–79)

The advance of the US 2nd Armored Division during the first day of Operation *Queen* forced the 7th Army to commit its available reserve, the 9th Panzer Division, supported by King Tigers of s.Pz.Abt. 506. The first elements of the division, commanded by Maj D. Bockhoff, arrived on November 17 and consisted of I./PGR 11 supported by about 25–30 Panther and King Tiger tanks. Kampfgruppe Bockhoff began attacking towards Puffendorf in the early morning hours. Task Force 1 of the 2nd Armored Division including tanks of the 1st and 2nd Battalion, 67th Armored were deployed in open ground and bore the brunt of the attack. The weather that day was overcast, and the ground was covered with mud and slush from the previous days of cold rain and light snow. The M4 tanks (1) had a hard time maneuvering in the mud, and their 76mm gun was largely ineffective against the thick frontal armor of the Panther medium tank (2) at long ranges. The experienced Panther crews attempted to maintain a safe distance from the US tanks, as their long-barreled 75mm gun could penetrate the thinner armor of the M4 tank at ranges of over 1,000 yards (1,000m). One M4A1 (76mm) fired 14 rounds of 76mm ammunition at a Panther before finally getting a hit on the thinner side armor. The German tanks attempted to take advantage of the ruins of local buildings for cover during the engagement, as seen here. The one-sided exchange ended later in the morning when TF1 was ordered to withdraw into the outskirts of Puffendorf, to take advantage of the protection offered by the local buildings. By this time tank losses had been heavy, with the 2nd Battalion having lost 19 tanks to German tank gunfire. After TF1 withdrew, the German Kampfgruppe attempted to restart its counterattack against the town, and the Panzers began to move forward over the contested ground. This exposed them to US tank gunfire and four Panzers were knocked out, two to 76mm tank fire and two more to 90mm fire from the M36 90mm GMC of the 702nd Tank Destroyer Battalion. The German infantry was pounded by US artillery and the Kampfgruppe was forced to withdraw. Total German tank losses during the day's fighting were 11 including one King Tiger from 3./s.Pz.Abt. 506, which was probably hit by an M36 tank destroyer. Like so much of the fighting along the Roer front, the outcome of the engagement was a stalemate, with both sides having suffered significant losses. However, the initiative remained with the 2nd Armored Division, which over the next few days battered its way towards the Roer, in spite of the fierce resistance of their old foes in the 9th Panzer Division.

An M8 armored car of the 17th Cavalry Group, passes the wreck of a German StuG III assault gun from Panzergrenadier Division 3 in Kinzweiller, Germany on November 21, 1944. The town was taken on November 19 by the 117th Infantry Regiment, 30th Division. (NARA)

town. The division's toll in Operation *Queen* was light compared with other divisions, 1,220 casualties.

The advance in the center by the 29th Division did not go as smoothly. Gen Gerhardt believed that tactics developed in Normandy would work best – attacking through the "weak spots" between the towns, and then reducing the towns afterwards. This proved to be fundamentally flawed, as was evident on the first day when battalions of the 115th and 175th Infantry quickly became pinned down by small-arms fire from the village strongpoints. Furthermore, Gerhardt was reluctant to deploy his supporting tank battalion into the "sea of mud," and so lacked a means to quickly overcome the town defenses. The 29th Division was rapidly falling behind its neighbors on either side, and after another day with little progress, Gerhardt was forced to admit that his tactics had failed. He accepted an offer from the neighboring 2nd Armored Division for tank support and planned a more vigorous use of the attached 747th Tank Battalion. On November 18, the division finally began to make broad progress along its front against the 246th VGD, finally taking Steerich, Bettendorf and the coalmine at Siersdorf, the initial layer of the Jülich defenses. With so few German reserves available in this sector, counterattacks were weak. The 81st Corps provided an assault gun battalion for a counterattack on November 19, but they were forced to withdraw by fighter-bomber strikes. By November 21, the 29th Division finally picked up steam and was within two kilometers of the Roer. The German 15th Army was very reluctant to commit its reserves, but the threat to the River Roer line was so great that Model freed up the 340th VGD, which had been sequestered for the Ardennes offensive. By this stage the 246th VGD had been reduced to only about 820 men in its three infantry regiments, and so it was pulled out. The insertion of fresh infantry from the 340th VGD halted the 29th Division's advance on November 22. Unlike its neighboring divisions, which consolidated their positions for several days after November 22, the 29th Division kept up a steady series of attacks towards Jülich. Bourheim was finally captured on November 23, but the 175th Infantry there was subjected to three

During Operation *Queen*, British Churchill Crocodile flamethrower tanks of Squadron B, 1st Fife and Forfar Yeomanry were attached to the 2nd Armored Division to aid in assaults against strongpoints on November 20–22. Mud was the main obstacle, and here an M4A3 (76mm) tank is seen providing cover for a Crocodile ahead of it, which has just flamed a German position. (NARA)

days of counterattacks and artillery shelling, averaging over 2,000 rounds per day. The neighboring 116th Infantry captured Koslar and was hit by the same pattern of repeated artillery strikes and counter-attacks. The German 81st Corps staged a co-ordinated counterattack by the 340th VGD on both villages on November 26, supported by 28 tanks and assault guns. The attacks broke into both villages but a sudden change in the weather allowed Allied fighter-bombers to intervene, smothering the German attacks. Nevertheless, two companies of the 116th Infantry were surrounded in Koslar and had to be resupplied by air. While the Germans were distracted by the fighting in Bourheim and Koslar, the 29th Division launched its third regiment, the 115th, against the last of the major towns in the Jülich defensive belt, securing Kirchberg on November 27. After a pause, the division pushed up to the edge of the River Roer in the first week of December. This final action was impeded by the extensive mining of the flat ground along the edge of the Roer. Swept by machine-gun fire, the advance over the exposed fields proved very costly, and after six days of fighting, the 116th Infantry was too battered to proceed. The 115th Infantry followed, finally pushing across the beaten ground northwest of Jülich and taking the city's Sportplatz after a very stiff fight. By December 9, the 29th Division had cleared the western bank of the Roer up to the city of Jülich.

The 2nd Armored Division formed the left wing of the XIX Corps assault, aimed at Gereonsweiler and Linnich. Its sector was so narrow that on November 16 the attacking force was limited to the CCB. The advance proceeded well in spite of the mud as the division had taken the precaution of fitting its tank tracks with "duck-bills" for better flotation in the mud as well as log mats to help extract tanks that became bogged down. Antitank defenses around Apweiler proved to be especially intense, but CCB made good progress. Indeed, the rapid loss of Puffendorf so alarmed German commanders that Rundstedt consented to the release of the only mechanized theater reserves available – the 9th Panzer Division and 15th PGD, supported by the s.Pz.Abt. 506 with 36 King Tiger tanks. This force immediately counterattacked on November 17, hitting Task

A disabled Panther of the 9th Panzer Division is towed away through Gereonsweiler by an M25 prime mover following the intense battles with the 2nd Armored Division in November 1944.

Force 1 near Puffendorf with PGR 11 supported by about 30 tanks. Caught out in the open, and outranged by the Panther's 75mm gun, TF1 was forced to pull back into Puffendorf. The tank fighting led to the loss of about 11 Panzers, but US losses were heavier. A renewed attack on Apweiler by TF2 also encountered the Panzer reinforcements and forced the attack back to the start line. The 2nd Armored Division commander, Gen Harmon, decided to commit part of CCA to the fray, but the presence of antitank ditches and a heavy concentration of fire from German tanks sitting on the hills around Gereonsweiler made it impossible for CCA to move forward. By the end of the day, the division had lost 18 M4 tanks destroyed and 16 more damaged along with 19 light tanks destroyed or damaged. The following day was spent supporting the neighboring 29th Division in the hope of securing the road network around Setterich. Although the 9th Panzer Division tried to counter-attack, the good flying weather filled the air with US fighter-bombers, which discouraged any large Panzer attacks. Harmon was an experienced tank commander who realized that sending his tanks across the muddy fields in direct view of the German tanks and antitank guns was suicidal. Instead, he decided to try to force the Germans out of Apweiler using the attached 406th Infantry from the 102nd Division. On the afternoon of November 18, the town was hit by a short but sharp artillery barrage followed very closely by 3/406th infantry, which quickly took the town. The Germans responded with a pre-dawn counterattack by a battalion of the 15th PGD, but it was crushed before it reached the town. After another day of fruitless skirmishes, the 2nd Armored Division launched its major attack on Gereonsweiler in the driving rain on November 20. The town was pummeled by artillery, then quickly overwhelmed by three task forces in the early afternoon. The predictable German counterattack was delayed until the next day and PGR 11 hit a company of the 406th Infantry very hard before finally being pushed back from the north side of the town.

The 2nd Armored Division's six-day battle to push out to the Roer had been one of the few clear successes of Operation *Queen*. In spite of

During fighting near Freialdenhoven on November 28, 1944, this King Tiger heavy tank from s.Pz.Abt. 506 was knocked out by M36 tank destroyers from the 702nd Tank Destroyer Battalion, 2nd Armored Division. The M36 was one of the few US AFVs that could successfully engage such a heavily armored foe. (NARA)

the miserable weather and exposed terrain, Harmon's skillful use of tanks and infantry had succeeded even in the face of strong counter-attacks by the only major German Panzer reserves in this sector. The attached 406th Infantry suffered 600 of the 1,300 casualties incurred, but had played a major role in securing several of the heavily defended strongpoints. Tank losses in 2nd Armored Division had been heavy, with about 75 knocked out or seriously damaged, but the division claimed 86 AFVs from the 9th Panzer Division and 15th PGD. As in the case of the 29th Division sector, German resistance stiffened on November 22 due to the arrival of reinforcements. As a result, the 2nd Armored Division halted major attacks to consolidate its gains and rebuild its strength before a final push to the Roer. The attack was renewed on November 26 along with the rest of the XIX Corps and reached the Roer on November 28.

For the XIX Corps, Operation *Queen* ended after three weeks with hopes for an easy breakthrough over the Roer dashed by stiff German resistance and the miserable weather. The corps suffered about 10,000 casualties, including 1,133 killed and 6,864 wounded. German casualties were significantly higher, with 8,321 prisoners and over 6,000 killed. Nevertheless, the Germans had managed to stymie a major American advance using a hodgepodge of battered divisions stiffened with occasional reinforcements.

OPERATION *CLIPPER*: VIII CORPS

Probably the most fearsome German defensive position in the Aachen sector apart from the Hürtgen forest was the town of Geilenkirchen, sitting on the River Wurm within a belt of Westwall bunkers. The town was in an awkward position for Allied planning too, as it sat astride the boundary between Bradley's 12th Army Group and Montgomery's 21st Army Group. As a result, the attack on Geilenkirchen was a combined British–US affaire

Geilenkirchen straddled the British and US sectors, so the British Shermans provided support for US infantry operations in the town, as seen here on November 19, 1944; the British Shermans are providing fire support for the US 84th Division. (NARA)

dubbed Operation *Clipper*, with the British 43rd Division assaulting the German positions north of Geilenkirchen, while the US 84th Division attacked from the south. The operation started two days later than Operation *Queen*, in the hope that the fighting elsewhere would draw off German reserves. German defenses around the town were significant, including the 176th Infantry Division north of the town and the 183rd VGD defending the town and the area towards the south. The attack of the 84th Division began in the predawn hours of November 18, with British searchlights bouncing off the low clouds to provide illumination for British flail tanks to sweep the minefields. The novice 334th Infantry received the support of British tanks for the remainder of the day and reached their objectives against moderate opposition. That night, a small but sharp German counterattack by PGR 10 supported by tanks hit the regiment near Prummern. The bunkers around Prummern were finally cleared the next day with the assistance of British Crocodile flamethrower tanks, and the 333rd Infantry joined the fray towards Geilenkirchen. The attacks the following day were greatly impeded by the heavy rains; the Crocodile flame tanks again proved very useful in clearing bunkers but eventually became bogged down in the mud. The slow pace of the advance was also the result of the commitment of the 15th PGD directly in the path of the 84th Division. Since the division was short one regiment, which was fighting alongside the 30th Division to the south, a regiment from the 102nd Division was added to the attack. Nevertheless, the attacks stalled against the reinforced German positions and further attacks were suspended on November 24 after the 84th Division had suffered 2,000 casualties.

The success of the neighboring 2nd Armored Division in taking Gereonweiler helped clear the Roer plains in front of Linnich. As a result, the long-planned insertion of Maj Gen Alvan Gillem's new VIII Corps was undertaken between the left flank of the XIX Corps and Geilenkirchen. It was hardly a full-strength corps at the time with only the 84th and 102nd divisions, both of which had detached regiments fighting on the XIX Corps front. During the lull in the fighting in the third week of November, Rundstedt correctly assessed that the British front in Holland was likely to remain dormant, so German units in that sector including the 10th SS-Panzer Division were shifted southward to the contested Roer sector. The new VIII Corps initiative was to push northward to the Roer by taking the heights in front of Lindern, and the attack began at dawn on November 29. The plan was to use surprise rather than artillery to break open the front, and a special detachment of troops of the 3/335th Infantry led the attack by infiltrating the Germans' defenses along the Gereonsweiler–Lindern road. Only about 100 soldiers made it through the defensive perimeter before the Germans opened fire, but the small band reached the outskirts of Lindern and held back several counterattacks during the day before reinforcements arrived late in the day. The Germans were so surprised by the lunge for Lindern that they only managed to cobble together a Kampfgruppe the next day using elements of the 9th and 10th SS-Panzer divisions, and King Tiger tanks of s.Pz.Abt. 506. Although the US penetration into Lindern was remarkably narrow, attacks along other portions of the VIII Corps front prevented the Germans from overwhelming the salient. The 102nd Division kept up a determined attack towards Linnich, finally breaking into the town on December 1. The 340th VGD holding this sector was finally pulled back for quick refitting after having been bloodied in the fighting for Jülich and Linnich, and it was replaced by the 363rd VGD from Holland. The needs for the upcoming Ardennes offensive again intervened, with Army Group B swapping infantry divisions for Panzer divisions. This process weakened the defenses facing the 84th Division, which finally pushed beyond Lindern. By the end of November, the new VIII Corps had not quite reached the Roer except at Linnich, but had pushed beyond the Siegfried Line.

OPERATION *QUEEN*: THE DECEMBER CLEAN UP

Of the four corps taking part in Operation *Queen*, three had reached most of their objectives along the River Roer. Curiously enough, it was the main push by Collins' VII Corps that had failed to meet its objective, due in no small measure to the intractability of the Hürtgen defenses. As a result, Collins called a halt to the VII Corps operations on December 7 to permit reorganization. Two of the four divisions committed to the Hürtgen, the 1st and 4th Infantry divisions, were burnt out and badly in need of rehabilitation away from the line. The 4th Infantry Division was replaced by the 83rd Division, while the 1st was replaced by the veteran 9th Division, which had been rebuilt after its own struggle in the Hürtgen in October. The aim of this final series of actions was to push the VII Corps conclusively out of the Hürtgen up to the edge of the Roer and the key city of Düren. To the south, the 83rd Division was tasked with the final push out of the Hürtgen through Gey, while to the north the 9th Division was tasked with pushing beyond the corner of the Hürtgen near Langerwehe on to the Roer plains beyond. The offensive resumed on December 10. The forces opposing the VII Corps were primarily

THE FINAL PUSH: VII CORPS REACHES THE ROER
DECEMBER 10–16, 1944

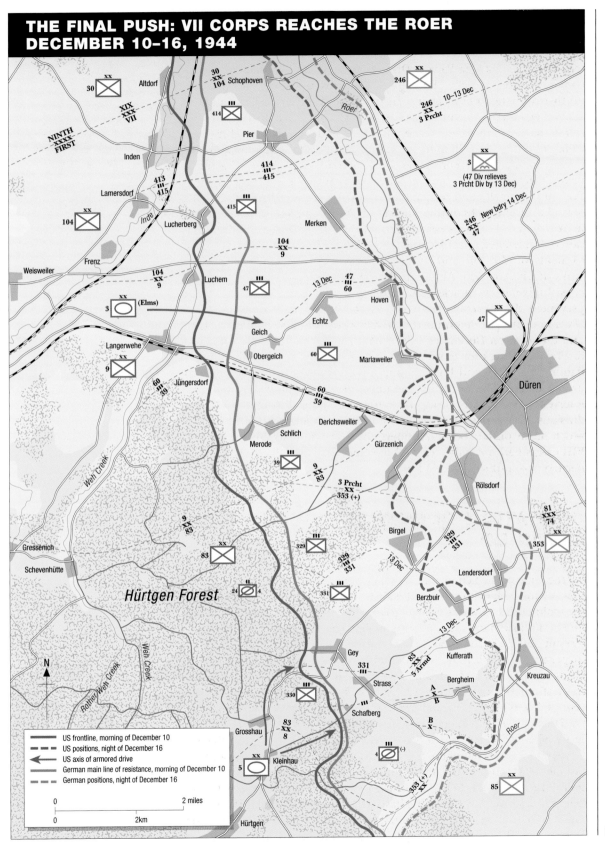

30 · Altdorf
Schophoven
30 / XXX / 104
XIX / XXX / VII
246
246 / XX / 3 Prcht · 10–13 Dec
414 · Pier
NINTH / XXXX / FIRST
Inden
3 · (47 Div relieves 3 Prcht Div by 13 Dec)
413 / 415 · Lamersdorf
414 / 415
104 · Merken
415
246 / XX / 47 · New bdry 14 Dec
Lucherberg
Weisweiler · Frenz
104 / XX / 9
104 / XX / 9 · Luchem
47 / 60 · 13 Dec
Hoven
3 · (Elms)
Langerwehe
9
Geich
Echtz
60 · Obergeich
Mariaweiler
47
Jüngersdorf
60 / 39
60 / 39
Derichsweiler
Düren
Schlich
Merode
Gürzenich
39
9 / XX / 83
3 Prcht / XX / 353 (+)
Rölsdorf
9 / XX / 83
Birgel
329 / 331
81 / XXX / 74
Gressenich
83
329
329 / 331 · 13 Dec
353
Schevenhütte
Lendersdorf
24 / 4
331
Berzbur
Hürtgen Forest
Weh Creek
13 Dec
Weh Creek
Gey
Kufferath
83 / XX / 5 Armd
N
331
Strass
Bergheim
Kreuzau
330
A / B
Rother Weh Creek
Schafberg
B
83 / XX / 8
Roer
Grosshau
4 / (-)
5 · Kleinhau
85
353 / XX

Legend
— US frontline, morning of December 10
- - - US positions, night of December 16
← US axis of armored drive
— German main line of resistance, morning of December 10
- - - German positions, night of December 16

0 ———— 2 miles
0 ———— 2km

Hürtgen

Köchling's 81st Corps with the 246th VGD north of Düren, the 3rd Fallschirmjäger Division defending Düren and its approaches, and the 353rd VGD to the south of the city. The German strength lay more in its potent artillery than in its battered infantry.

In the north, the 104th Division continued its assault out of the River Inde area, and within four days pushed the 246th VGD back to the Roer. The attack in the center by the 9th Infantry Division was supported by armor from the 3rd Armored Division and made slow progress at first. The division attacked with all three regiments: the 47th Infantry to the north, the 60th Infantry in the center, and the 39th making the turn southward to clear out the towns along the eastern edge of the Hürtgenwald. By this stage, the 3rd Fallschirmjäger Division was in little position to resist, but attempts to replace it with the weakly rebuilt 47th VGD did not provide enough strength to hold on to the towns west of Düren. Within four days the 9th Division reached its objectives. Total casualties in the three divisions taking part had been 1,074, including 179 killed.

The 83rd Division had the unenviable task of pushing through the final portion of the Hürtgen forest to reach the towns of Gey, and Strass. The division decided to conduct a night advance through the woods to minimize the risk of German artillery, and, despite the usual assortment of minefields and obstacles, two infantry battalions reached the outskirts of Gey and Strass by dawn on December 10. The towns were stubbornly defended by the 353rd VGD, and attempts to move up tanks to assist in the attack on Gey floundered due to the mud and minefields. In contrast, the arrival of a platoon of tanks at Strass helped ensure its fall before dusk. The German infantry infiltrated into the village of Schafberg that night, essentially cutting off the US infantry battalion in Strass and setting the stage for several counterattacks against Strass on December 11. The main push by the division came on December 14, when the road situation had improved to the point that the 83rd Division could be supported by two combat commands of the 5th Armored Division. The 329th Infantry pushed out of the woods and took Gürzenich, while the 331st Infantry overcame a battalion of the 47th VGD in Birgel. Although the CCB, 5th Armored Division had a hard time moving beyond Strass, a rapid advance by CCA on Kufferath forced the defenses in the CCB sector to fold. By December 16, the VII Corps had reached the Roer, the same day the German offensive in the Ardennes struck the neighboring V Corps. The month-long fight from the launch of Operation *Queen* to December 16 had cost the VII Corps 15,908 battle casualties, including 2,448 killed as well as 8,550 non-battle casualties. The heaviest losses had been suffered by the 104th Division though this was in part due to the fact that it was the only division actively committed every day of the offensive.

THE PRELUDE TO THE ARDENNES

With US forces approaching the Roer, the issue of the Roer dams took on a new urgency. The ferocity of the fighting in the Hürtgen raised the possibility that the dams would not be taken in time, so Eisenhower's SHAEF headquarters raised the issue with the RAF, which had breached the Ruhr dams in 1943. Air Chief Marshal Sir Arthur Harris was not optimistic: the big Schwammenauel dam was an earthen dam, and thus not easily breached. In spite of this, attacks began in early December by the RAF without any perceptible effect; they were halted in the middle of the month by bad weather and the start of the Ardennes offensive.

Hodges began to take steps to renew the ground attack towards the dams, giving the task to Gerow's V Corps. Four divisions were to take part: the 8th Infantry Division from its perch on the Brandenberg–Bergstein ridge, the fresh 78th Division through the Monshau forest, and the 2nd Infantry Division and elements of the new 99th Division in the forested area where the Ardennes and Eifel begin to blend into the Monschau forest. Facing them were stretches of the Westwall bunkers defended by the 272nd and 277th VG divisions. The German defenses were in a state of flux, since these two divisions were scheduled to be replaced in order to participate in the Ardennes offensive. Although the initial attacks on December 13 caught the Germans by surprise, resistance stiffened immediately, especially facing the 2nd Infantry Division around Wahlerscheid. Unknown to V Corps, they had stumbled into the reinforced divisions preparing to launch their own attacks as part of the German Ardennes offensive on December 16.

The launch of Operation *Wacht am Rhein* in the Ardennes on December 16 put a quick end to the Roer fighting. The Wehrmacht struck with two armies against the V Corps' five divisions in the Ardennes. The attack focused around Dietrich's 6th Panzer Army's drive towards the Losheim gap, which contained the bulk of the Waffen-SS Panzer divisions. It was poorly led and quickly became bogged down when faced by a tenacious defense around Krinkelt–Rocherath by elements of the 99th Division and 2nd Infantry Division, and that at St Vith by elements of the 7th Armored Division. Manteuffel's 5th Panzer Army showed considerably more skill, even if not endowed with the resources of the 6th Panzer Army. This force included units bloodied in the Siegfried Line fighting, the refreshed 9th and 116th Panzer divisions. The 5th Panzer Army crushed the newly arrived 106th Division, and battered the 28th Division, which was still recuperating from the Hürtgen fighting. Nevertheless, the stalwart defense by the 28th Division on the approaches

A pair of Jagdpanzer 38 assault guns of Panzerjäger Abteilung 272 were disabled along Hauptstrasse in Kesternich during the bitter fighting in December 1944 between the 272nd VGD and the US 78th Division, in the days before the outbreak of the Ardennes offensive. (NARA)

to Bastogne slowed the German advance long enough for the 12th Army Group to rush in reinforcements. The only theater reserves, the 82nd and 101st Airborne divisions, were hastily dispatched to Belgium, while the First Army rushed the 2nd and 3rd Armored divisions to stop the spearheads of the 5th Panzer Army before they reached the River Meuse. Patton's Third Army, on the verge of staging Operation *Tink* aimed at Frankfurt, quickly reoriented their attack northward and reinforced Bastogne by Christmas. The Battle of the Bulge lasted well into the middle of January, as the US Army gradually pushed the Wehrmacht from the Ardennes back to their starting points in the Eifel.

The Battle of the Bulge crippled the Wehrmacht in the west. In January 1945, the Red Army launched its main offensive over the River Oder, rumbling towards Berlin. Priority for troops and equipment shifted back to the Russian Front, and the Wehrmacht in the west made do with the leftovers. With the Bulge cleared, the Allied offensive in western Germany was renewed in February. Some of the Roer dams were opened by the Wehrmacht on February 9–10, which delayed operations along the Roer during the middle of February. The Roer dams were finally captured; the Schwammenauel dam was taken on February 10. Once the water receded, the US Army advance rapidly picked up momentum. The Roer was crossed on a broad front by the end of February, and Hodges' First Army was the first across the Rhine at Remagen on March 7, followed by Patton's Third Army a week later.[3]

3 For further details, see Osprey Campaign 175: *Rcmagen 1945*.

THE CAMPAIGN IN RETROSPECT

The Siegfried Line campaign in the autumn of 1944 was one of the most costly fought by the US Army during World War II, with about 48,000 battle casualties including at least 8,250 killed in action. About half these casualties were incurred in the Hürtgenwald. The rationale for the bloody push into the Hürtgen was confused, and the conduct of the campaign was clumsy. As an attritional campaign, it mauled six German divisions and hampered German efforts to rebuild its forces prior to the Ardennes offensive. The Wehrmacht lost over 12,000 killed in the forest fighting and many more prisoners and wounded. The forest fighting favored the defender, and the Germans were able to hold the First Army at bay with an assortment of second- and third-rate units. German commanders later argued that Hodges' concern over the threat posed by the Hürtgen to the right flank of VII Corps was unfounded as they lacked the strength to attack through the forest. Yet the Hürtgen fighting had unanticipated consequences. Gen Maj G. von Gersdorf, chief of staff of the German 7th Army, believed that the Hürtgen fighting had profound and seldom recognized effects in undermining the later German offensive in the neighboring Ardennes, stating that in his opinion the Hürtgenwald fighting "was one of the primary reasons for the failure of the (Ardennes) offensive by the German right wing. The Hürtgenwald clear of (American) forces and under German control would have enabled us to start the offensive with quite a different impetus. Since the (right wing) was the center of gravity in the Ardennes offensive, the Hürtgenwald evidently was one of the decisive factors leading to the failure of this operation." From a narrower tactical perspective, the Hürtgen portion of Operation *Queen* was a failure. The First Army was unable to exit the forest with enough strength to push on to Düren, and the offensive failed to solve the problem posed by the Roer dams.

The US Army operations in the Aachen corridor were more skillful and successful than the Hürtgenwald battles. Territorial gains were not particularly impressive – the deepest penetration into Germany by the First and Ninth armies after crossing the German frontier was only 22 miles. Yet Eisenhower's limited objective – to tie down the Wehrmacht in an attritional battle until logistics were ready for a renewed offensive in 1945 – was accomplished. During the autumn fighting, the Wehrmacht lost 95,000 men to the First and Ninth armies in prisoners alone, and other battle casualties were comparable to US losses.

The Wehrmacht's record was likewise rather mixed. The ability of the Wehrmacht to rebuild after the "void" of late August and early September 1944 was rightly dubbed the "miracle of the west." Rundstedt's and Model's skill at delaying the American advance with an absolute minimum of reinforcements was a testament to their tactical skills. On the other hand, the Siegfried Line campaign hinted at the continued lack of strategic perspective of the Wehrmacht since its abdication of decision-making to Hitler. The slow, deliberate retreat of the Wehrmacht only served to ensure the desolation of German cities and towns by the superior firepower of the Allies. The final year of the war would be far more costly to the German civilian population than the previous four years of the war combined, and would leave Germany in ruins. The cruel paradox of war was that in defending Germany, the Wehrmacht merely served to ensure its devastation.

THE BATTLEFIELDS TODAY

Germany has had little reason to memorialize the horrible battles of the autumn of 1944, and few monuments or museums exist to commemorate the bitter 1944 fighting. There is a small museum to the Hürtgen fighting in Vossenack and a small memorial to the 116th Panzer Division in neighboring Simonskall. There are at least six German military cemeteries in the Hürtgenwald and the Soldatenfriedhof Vossenack also includes the grave of GFM Model, who committed suicide rather than surrender after the encirclement of Army Group B in the Ruhr pocket in April 1945.

The concrete fortifications of the Westwall are one of the few durable reminders of the war, but, even in this case, they have been much more thoroughly obliterated than the German fortifications along the Altlantic coast. In recent years, more interest has been shown in this aspect of Germany's forgotten past, and an archeological survey of the Westwall in the Aachen area found that fewer than 10 percent of the fortifications still survive. Most of these bunkers are relatively small and overgrown, so locating them can be a challenge without a guidebook. The dragon's teeth, so characteristic of the Westwall, are thoroughly hated by local farmers and most have been removed. Hans-Josef Hansen's book *Auf den Spuren des Westwalls* takes at look at the contemporary impact of the remaining Westwall.

Some larger structures connected with the Aachen fighting survive – for example, the air-raid shelter (*Zivilschutzbunker*) on Lütticherstrasse. The Hürtgenwald has returned to peace as a state nature sanctuary, and the German government expended a considerable amount of time and effort in the late 1940s and early 1950s to clean up the remaining mines and war debris. The dirt road through the Kall ravine is little changed since the war, and, for those interested in visiting, the article in *After the Battle* magazine by Karel Magry (Number 71, 1991) is an excellent guide to help discover what remains of the forest fighting.

FURTHER READING

The person most closely associated with chronicling the Siegfried Line campaign was Charles MacDonald, a young company commander at the time and later a US Army historian. He was the author not only of the official US Army "Green Book" history of the campaign, but also the author of the classic account of the Hürtgen fighting, as well as the chapter in the US Army special study that covered the fighting of the 28th Division at Schmidt. Another essential account is the more recent book by Robert Rush, which provides an insightful look at one of the regiments of the US 4th Infantry Division in the Hürtgen as well as its German opponents. The German perspective on the campaign can be found in reports prepared by German officers for the US Army Office of Military History as part of the Foreign Military Studies effort, and these can be found at the US Army Military History Institute at Carlisle Barracks, Pennsylvania. Although it does not cover the section of the Westwall covered in this book, the French Army study by Capt De Beaurepaire *À l'assaut de la Ligne Siegfried* is an exceptional study of the construction of a section of the Westwall in the Palatinate and also covers the tactics used by US and French units of the 6th Army Group to assault it on March 18–25, 1945.

US Army Foreign Military Studies

Bork, Max *The 47th Volksgrenadier Division in the West* (B-602).
Denkert, Walter *The 3rd Pz Gren Div in the Battle of Aachen October 1944* (A-979).
Engel, Gerhard *First Battle of Aachen 16–22 September 1944* (A-971).
Engel, Gerhard *The 12th Infantry Div in the 3rd Battle of Aachen, 16 November–3 December 1944* (B-764).
Gersdorff, Rudolf *The Battle of the Hürtgen Forest, November–December 1944* (A-891).
Köchling, Friedrich *The Battle of the Aachen Sector* (A-989 to A-998).
Schack, Friedrich *LXXXI Corps, 4–21 September 1944* (B-816).
Straube, Erich *The 74th Corps from September to December 1944* (C-016).
Toppe, Alfred *Units Opposing the 28th Division in the Hürtgen forest* (C-089).

US Army Studies

V Corps: *V Corps Operations in the ETO: 6 January 1942-9 May 1945* (1945).
XIX Corps: *Breaching the Siegfried Line/XIX Corps 2 October 1944* (1945).
US Army Armored School: *Armor in the Attack of Fortified Positions* (1950).
US Army Armored School: *Hell on Wheels in the Drive to the Roer: The Employment of the 2nd Armored Division in a Limited Objective Attack* (date unknown).
Gabel, Christopher "Knock 'em All Down: The Reduction of Aachen, October 1944," in *Block by Block: The Challenge of Urban Operations* (US Army Command and General Staff College, 2003).
Heichler, Lucian *The Germans opposite VII Corps in September 1944* (OCMH, 1952).

Published accounts

3rd Armored Division: *Spearhead in the West: The Third Armored Division* (1945; Battery Press reprint, 1980).

28th Infantry Division: *28th Infantry Division in World War II* (1945; Battery Press reprint, 2000).

Astor, Gerald *The Bloody Forest: Battle for the Huertgen* (Presidio, 2000).

Corlett, Charles *Cowboy Pete: The Autobiography of Maj. Gen. Charles Corlett* (Sleeping Fox, 1974).

Christoffel, Edgar *Krieg am Westwall 1944/45* (Interbook, 1989).

Egersdorfer, R. H. *Stolberg: Penetrating the Westwall* (26th Infantry Regiment Association, 1999)

Fuhrmeister, Jorg *Der Westwall: Geschichte und Gegenwart* (Motorbuch, 2003).

Gross, Mannfred et al *Der Westwall: Vom Denkmalwert des Unerfreulichen* (Rheinland-Verlag, 1997).

Guderian, Heinz Günther *From Normandy to the Ruhr with the 116th Panzer Division in WWII* (Aberjona, 2001).

Haasler, Timm *Den Westwall halten oder mit dem Westwall untergehen: Die Geschichte der Panzerbrigade 105* (Schneider, 2005).

Hansen, Hans-Josef *Auf den Spuren des Westwalls* (Helios, 2005).

Hogan, David *A Command Post at War: First Army HQ in Europe 1943–45* (US Army, 2000).

Hohenstein, Adolf and Trees, Wolfgang *Hölle im Hürtgenwald* (Triangel, 1981).

Kramp, Hans *Rurfront 1944/45* (self-published, 1981).

Kurowski, Franz *Hitler's Last Bastion: The Final Battle for the Reich 1944–45* (Schiffer, 1998).

MacDonald, Charles *The Battle of the Huertgen Forest* (Lippincott, 1963).

MacDonald, Charles *The Siegfried Line Campaign* (US Army, 1963).

MacDonald, Charles and Mathews, Sidney *Three Battles: Arnaville, Altuzzo, and Schmidt* (US Army, 1952).

Miller, Edward *A Dark and Bloody Ground: The Hürtgen Forest and the Roer River Dams 1944-45* (Texas A&M, 1995).

Rush, Robert *Hell in the Hürtgen Forest: The Ordeal and Triumph of an American Infantry Regiment* (University of Kansas Press, 2001).

Yeide, Harry *The Longest Battle: September 1944 to February 1945* (Zenith, 2005).

GLOSSARY AND ABBREVIATIONS

AFV	Armored fighting vehicle.
Army	Allied formation consisting of several corps.
Army Group	Formation consisting of several armies.
CC	Combat command of a US armored division; CCA, CCB or CCR.
Corps	Formation consisting of several divisions.
ETO	European Theater of Operations.
Gen	General.
GFM	Generalfeldmarschall (field marshal).
GR	Grenadier regiment.
IR	Infanterie regiment.
Lt	Lieutenant.
Maj	Major.
PGD	Panzergrenadier division.
PGR	Panzergrenadier regiment.
PzAA	Panzer Aufklärungs Abteilung (armored reconnaissance regiment).
s.Pz.Abt.	schwere Panzer Abteilung (heavy tank regiment).
TF	Task Force; sub-formation of a US combat command.
VGD	Volksgrenadier Division.

INDEX

Figures in **bold** refer to illustrations

Aachen
   defenses 14, 17–18, 31, 41
   first battle of 31–5
   second battle of **38–40**, 44–8, **44–8**
   Siegfried Line defenses 18–22, **19**
   strategic significance 27
air support, US
   dam-busting **88**, 89
   operations 36, 43, 63–4, 75, 76, 82, 83
   and weather 26, 43, 61
Allen, Gen "Terrible Terry" 64, 66
Alsdorf 41, 42, 46–7
Altdorf 77–81
Apweiler 82, 83
Ardennes campaign 29–30, 63, 65, 86, 89–90
Ardennes-Eifel front 31, 89
Arnhem *see* Operation *Market Garden*
artillery *see* weapons and artillery

Bardenburg 43, 46–7
Barton, Maj Gen Raymond "Tubby" 67, **68**, 74
Bergstein 57, 70–1, 76
Bettendorf 81
Birgel 88
Birk 43
Bourheim 77, 81–2
Bradley, Gen Omar 14, 28, 48–9, 60, 61, 67, 76
Brandenberg 70–1, 76
Brandenberger, Gen Erich 13, **13**, 14, 35, 37, 43
British/ Canadian forces 28, **82**, 85, **85**
Bulge, Battle of the 29–30, 63, 65, 86, 89–90
bunkers **11**, 20–2, **21–2**, **33**, 35–6, **54–6**

Collins, Maj Gen Lawton "Lightning Joe" 14–15, **15**, 34–5, 49, 64–5, 74, 86
Corlett, Maj Gen Charles "Cowboy Pete" 15, **15**, 35, 36–7
Cota, Maj Gen Norman 15, 58, 59, 60, **60**
Crucifix Hill 42

Daniel, Lt Col Derrill **38–40**
Davis, Brig Gen George 60
Dekert, Gen Maj Walter 43
Donnerberg 65
dragon's teeth **7**, **20**, **22**, **31–2**, 92
Düren 63, 64, 88

Eastern Front *see* Russian Front
Eisenhower, Gen Dwight D. 28, 48–9, **60**

Ellendorf 32
Engel, Gen Maj Gerhard **13**, 34
Eschweiler 64, 66

fortifications **11**, 20–2, **20–2**, **33**, **54–6**, 92
Freialdenhoven **84**
Frenzerburg 65
fuel 17, **27**, 29

Geich 7
Geilenkirchen 35, 63, 76–7, 84–5, **85**
Geisberg 32
Gereonsweiler 82, 83, **83**
Gerhardt, Gen 81
German Army: brigades
   Panzer 105 17
   Panzer 108 42, 43
   StuG 341 50–1, 58
   StuG 394 58
German Army: corps
   1st SS-Panzer 17
   74th 17, 52, 57
   81st 17–18, 33, 36–7, 41, 52, 63, 81, 82, 88
German Army: divisions
   3rd Fallschirmjäger 65, 66, 88
   3rd PGD 41–2, 43–4, 46–7, 63, 66, 77
   9th Panzer 17, 32, 34–5, **78–80**, 82–3, 84, 86, 89
   10th SS-Panzer 86
   12th Infantry 17–18, 33–4, **33**, 41, 63, 64, 65–6
   15th PGD 82–3, 84, 85
   46th Infantry 46–7
   47th VGD 63, 64, 65, 88
   49th Infantry 17, 41, 46–7
   89th Infantry 32–3, 50–1, 57–8, 59
   116th Panzer 17, 18, 33, 41–2, 43, 50–1, 57–61, 64, 89
   176th Infantry 85
   183rd VGD 18, 41, 85
   246th VGD 18, 41, 44–8, 63, 66, 81, 88
   272nd VGD 57, 70–1, 76, 89, 90
   275th 17, 18, 49, 53, 58, 67, 69, 70–1
   277th VGD 89
   340th VGD 81–2, 86
   344th VGD 69, 70–1
   353rd Infantry 17, 35, 70–1, 88
   363rd VGD 86
German Army: KGs
   Bayer 50–1
   Bockhoff **78–80**
   Diefenthal 43, 46–7
   Rink 45–8, **48**
German Army: regiments
   Fusilier 27 34
   GR 48 34

GR 104 64
GR 980 70–1, 76
GR 1055 50–1, 60
GR 1056 50–1, 59, 60
GR 1058 69
Mobile von Fritzchen 41, 42–3, 46–7
PGR 8 43
PGR 10 85
PGR 11 **78–80**, 83
PGR 29 43
PGR 60 43, 46–7, 57, 59
PGR 156 50–1, 57, 59
PR 16 50–1, 58
PzAA 116 57, 59, 60
Gerow, Maj Gen Leonard 14, **15**, 31, 60
Gersdorf, Gen Maj G. von 76, 91
Gey 70–1, 74, 86, 88
Grosshau 69–73, **75**
Gürzenich **23**, 88

Hamich 64
Harmon, Maj Gen Ernest 83, 84
Hill 187 65
Hill 194 44
Hill 203 65
Hitler, Adolf 11, 13, 14, 29, 31, 44
Hodges, Lt Gen Courtney 14, **14**, 15, 40, 49, 60, 89, 91
Hürtgen 69, 70–1, **73–4**, 74–5
Hürtgen forest
   defenses **54–6**
   first US attempts to clear 23–4, **23–4**, 32-3, 34–5, **42**, 48–61, **49–56**, **58**
   nowadays 92
   Operation *Queen* 63, 65, 67–76, **67–75**, 86–9
   in retrospect 91

Immendorf **77**
Inde River valley 65–6, 88
Inden 66

Jülich 64, 81, 82
Jüngersdorf 65

Kall ravine 50–1, **52**, 57, **58**, 59, 60–1, 92
Kesternich **90**
Kinzweiller **81**
Kirchberg 57, 82
Kleinhau 70–1, **72**, 73, 75
Köchling, Gen 36, 37
Kohlscheid 44
Kommerscheidt 50–1, 57, 58–9, 60–1
Kornelimunster 32
Koslar 82

Langerwehe 65, **66**, 86
Lanham, Col Charles **68**

Lindern 86
Linnich 82, 85–6
logistics 12, **27**, 30, 82
Lucherberg 66
Luftwaffe 16, 76

Marienberg 36
Merode 65
Mestrenger Mill 50–1, 59
Model, GFM Walter **13**
  death 92
  and operations 41–2, 43, 52, 57, 63,
    76, 81, 91–2
  overview 13
Monschau forest 32, 89
Montgomery, FM Bernard 11, 28, 48–9

Nothberg 65

Operation
  Bagration 13
  Clipper 84–6
  Market Garden 11, 28, 35
  Queen 49, 61–84, 86–9

Palenberg 36
Peterson, Col Carl 57, 58
Prummern 85
Puffendorf tank battle **78–80**, 82–3

Rabenheck ridge 68, 70–1
RAF 63, 88, 89
Ravels Hill 42, 43, 46–7
Rimburg 36
Roer River
  dams 53, 57, 67, 75–6, **88**, 89, 90
  and operations 32, 49, 61, 63–6
  strategic significance 30
  US reaches 81–9
Ruhr industrial region 27
Rundstedt, GFM Gerd von 13, 14, 37,
  65, 66, 82, 86, 91–2
Russian Front 11, 13, 28–9, 90

Schack, Gen 33–4
Schafberg 88
Scharnhorst Line **7**, 20, 31, **31–2**, 35–6
Scheldt estuary 12
Schevenhütte 32, **33**, 34
Schill Line 20, 32–3, 42, 57
Schmidt 50-1, 52, 57, 58–9
Schwammenauel Reservoir and dam
  53, 89, 90
Schwerin, Gen Lt Graf Gerhard von
  13–14, **14**
Setterich 83
Siegfried Line
  defenses 18–22, **19**
  see also fortifications; Scharnhorst
  Line; Schill Line
Siersdorf 81
Starkey, Pvt Robert **64**
Steerich 81
Stolberg 66
Stolberg corridor 32, 34–5, **34**, 61,
  63–6
Strass 88–9

tactics
  bunker-busting 35–6
  forest fighting 53, 56
  urban assault **38–40**, **44**
  US artillery 25
tank destroyers **38–40**, 84
tanks
  Churchill Crocodile flamethrowers
    82
  German shortage 17, 41
  King Tigers **84**
  M4 **6–7**, 24, **33**, **36**, **38–40**, 73–4,
    78–80
  M4A3 **82**
  M4A3E2 **66**
  mud matting **61**
  Panthers **77–80**, **83**
  Pzkpfw IV **64**
  Shermans **85**
  US organization and strength 24–5
Thimister **9**
trenches **54–6**

Ubach 36, **36–7**, 37
US Army
  armored divisions 24–5
  engineers **31**, **37**
  Rangers 70–1, 76
  replacement policy 23
US Army: corps
  V 31, 49–61, 61–2, 67–76, 88–90
  VII 31–5, 42, 43–4, 46–7, 61, 63–6,
    86–9
  VIII 84–6
  XIX 35–44, 46–7, 76–84
US Army: divisions
  1st Infantry 32, 42, 43–4, 46–7, 63,
    64–5, 86
  2nd Armored 24, 35, 37, 43, 46–7,
    77, **77**, **78–80**, 81, 82–4, 90
    CCA 41, 83
    CCB 37, 82–3
  2nd Infantry 89
  3rd Armored **7**, 24, 25, **31**, **33**, 88, 90
    CCA 32, 64, 65
    CCB 32, 64
  4th 22–3, 60, 63, 67–74, **67**, **69**, **73**,
    86
  5th Armored 31, 88
    CCA 74, 88–9
    CCB 88–9
    CCR 70–1, 74–5
  7th Armored 89
  8th Infantry 69, 70–1, 72–3, 74–6,
    89
  9th **6**, 32–3, **32**, 34–5, **42**, 49, **61**, 86,
    88
  28th 49-61, **49**, 89–90
  29th 43, 77–82, 83
  30th 35, 36–41, **41**, 42–4, 46–7,
    77–81
  78th 89, 90
  82nd 90
  83rd 70–1, 74, 86, 88–9
  84th 77, 85, 86
  99th 89
  101st Airborne 90
  102nd 85, 86
  104th 64, 65–6, 88, 89
  106th 89
US Army: regiments
  8th Infantry 67–8, **67**, 69–73

  12th Infantry 60, 67, 72
  13th Infantry 75
  16th Infantry 32, 65
  18th Infantry 42, 43, 46–7, 65
  22nd 22–3, 67, 68–73, **73**
  26th **38–40**, 44–8, 65
  39th Infantry **32**, 88
  47th Infantry 65, 88
  60th **6**, 88
  67th Armored **36**, **78–80**
  109th 50–1, 52, 53, 60
  110th 50–1, 52, 53–7, 59
  112th 50–1, 52, 57–61
  115th 81, 82
  116th Infantry 43, 82
  117th 36, 41, **41**, 42, 44, 46–7, 77
  119th 36, 37, 43, 44, 46–7
  120th Infantry 43, 44, 46–7
  121st Infantry 70–1, 74
  175th 81–2
  329th Infantry 88
  331st Infantry 88
  333rd Infantry 85
  334th Infantry 85
  335th Infantry 86
  406th Infantry 83, 84
  413th Infantry 66
  414th Infantry 66
  415th Infantry 66
US army: task forces
  Boyer 70–1
  Hamberg 70–1, 75–6
  Hogan 48
  Richardson 65
  Ripple 50–1, 59

vehicles
  Earthworm minerollers **75**
  half-tracks **48**, **74**
  jeeps **25**
  M8 armored cars **81**
  M25 prime movers **83**
  M29 Weasels **25**
  trucks **27**
Verlautenheide 34, 42, 43
Vicht 32
Vossenack 50–1, 52, 57–8, 59–61, 92

Wahlerscheid 89
weapons and artillery
  ammunition supplies 15, 25, 63
  antitank **18**, 21, 24, **41**, **45**, 63, **72**
  artillery in Hürtgen forest 23–4
  artillery in Würselen area 77
  assault guns **81**, **90**
  bazookas **41**, **64**
  flamethrowers **23**
  German artillery 37–41
  GMCs **23**, 35–6, **53**, **68**, **75**
  HMGs **41**
  howitzers **42**
  M1 Garand rifles **65**
  mortars **73**
  rocket artillery **72**
  US field artillery 25
Weisser Weh ravine 68, 70–1
Wilde Sau minefield 53, 70–1, 74–5
Wilck, Col Gerhard 44–8, **48**
Wurm River 36
Würselen 42–3, 44, 46–7, 77